AF328669

Praise for *Calling All Heroes*

"Calling All Heroes is exactly what our fundraising community needs right now. Tammy Zonker offers an empathetic and thoughtful guide to moving past the binary thinking that surrounds the typical donor-centric vs. community-centric dialogue. She skillfully balances donor relationships with community impact, encouraging us to approach our work with deeper curiosity, humility, and collaboration. If you're committed to a more ethical, inclusive, and effective philanthropy, this book will feel like an empowering and timely resource."

—Mallory Erickson
Creator of Practivated and Power Partners Formula™,
Author of What the Fundraising—Embracing and Enabling the
People Behind the Purpose

"Driving fundraising growth requires a unique personal blend of two values, which one must master simultaneously—idealism and pragmatism. Tammy blends these exquisitely in this book and moves beyond the emotions about donor- and community-centred fundraising from the various lobbies, to systematically show how these two philosophies can be successfully blended for the common good. This book takes abstract concepts and turns them into specific, measurable actions. Well done Tammy!"

—Alan Clayton
Chair at Revolutionise International and Author,
Great Fundraising Organizations

"In these especially challenging times for fundraisers and changemakers globally, Tammy Zonker's new tour de force book, "Calling All Heroes" has effectively created a new paradigm of Human-Centered Fundraising. By bringing together, for the first time, the very best of Ken Burnett's donor-centered "Relationship Fundraising" with community-centered fundraising, Tammy has developed a manifesto with a powerful call to action for the nonprofit sector, if it wants to not only survive but to grow. This must-read book draws on our rich fundraising journey, highlights impactful case studies, and identifies the opportunities and potential pitfalls along the way, whilst providing a clear roadmap for those fundraising heroes ready to make the next big positive change in fundraising. Be human, be that change!"

—Daryl Upsall
FCIOF, President—Daryl Upsall International

"Tammy Zonker's Calling All Heroes is the rallying cry our sector needs. She brilliantly bridges donor-centered and community-centered approaches into a powerful, human-centered model that prioritizes empathy, equity, and collaboration. As a fellow fundraiser and changemaker, I fully endorse her message and believe this book will reshape how we think about impact."

—Ken Miller
CFRE, Author, Speaker, and Consultant

"Tammy Zonker reminds us that the real magic of fundraising happens when we stop taking sides and start taking responsibility. We don't need more jargon or judgment—we need frameworks that help us think clearly and act courageously. Tammy delivers exactly that. Calling All Heroes is wise, generous, and exactly what the sector needs right now."

—T. Clay Buck
CFRE, Founder & Principal, Next River Fundraising Strategies

"Tammy Zonker has nailed it. In a fundraising world divided between "community based" and "donor centred" fundraising, Zonker finds the middle ground in a new paradigm she labels "human-centred" fundraising. Her value-driven approach and her extensive lived-experience give rise to practical suggestions and specific actions to prepare the reader to thrive in a world of continuous disruption. Her writing explodes with Zonker's passion for her craft and the practice of philanthropy. Zonker's profound love for the social impact sector, the people who serve in it, and those served by it shines through in every chapter."

—Tony Myers
CEO, Leaders of Tomorrow Canada Foundation,
Edmonton/Calgary, Canada

"A compelling vision for our time. With passion, insight and wisdom, Tammy Zonker reveals a transformative path that will make a positive difference to non-profits, our communities and our future. If you want meaningful change, buy this book. Read it. Follow the advice. And watch your community be transformed for the better."

—Harvey McKinnon
President, Harvey McKinnon Associates and Co-author of
The Power of Giving: How Giving Back Enriches Us All. Author of
The Healthy Nonprofit, How to Create Lifelong Donors Through Monthly Giving,
Hidden Gold, and The 11 Questions Every Donor Asks

"Community-centered (born circa 2019) or donor-centered fundraising (adopted as a communications tactic in 1993)? Which is best for your nonprofit? Good news. Turns out: community- and donor-centered fundraising are fully compatible, now that we have some proof. Your charity can act equitably and ethically in its community role . . . while keeping your fundraising on boil. Expert Tammy Zonker lays out the principles in her fast, up-to-the-minute new book, Calling All Heroes."

—Tom Ahern
Award-winning copywriter and author. The New York Times called
Tom Ahern, "One of the country's most sought-after creators of
fund-raising messages."

"Tammy Zonker doesn't just talk equity—she builds a bridge between power, purpose, and people. Calling All Heroes is the rally cry our sector needs—it's a courageous invitation to build fundraising practices that are bold, inclusive, and deeply human. If you care about justice, dignity, and raising serious money without compromising your values, this book belongs on your desk."

— Dana Synder
Founder of Positive Equation and Author of The Monthly Giving Mastermind

CALLING
ALL
Heroes

COMBINING THE BEST OF DONOR-CENTERED AND COMMUNITY-CENTERED FUNDRAISING FOR GREATER IMPACT

TAMMY ZONKER

WILEY

Library of Congress Cataloging-in-Publication Data

Names: Zonker, Tammy, author.
Title: Calling all heros : combining the best of donor-centered and
   community-centered fundraising for greater impact / Tammy Zonker.
Description: Hoboken, New Jersey : Wiley, [2026] | Includes index.
Identifiers: LCCN 2025033034 (print) | LCCN 2025033035 (ebook) | ISBN
   9781394338597 (hardback) | ISBN 9781394338610 (adobe pdf) | ISBN
   9781394338603 (epub)
Subjects: LCSH: Nonprofit organizations—Finance. | Fund raising.
Classification: LCC HG4027.65 .Z66 2026 (print) | LCC HG4027.65 (ebook)
LC record available at https://lccn.loc.gov/2025033034
LC ebook record available at https://lccn.loc.gov/2025033035

Cover Design: Wiley
Cover Image: © Designer_things/Getty Images
Author Photo: R. Trent Thompson

Printed and bound by CPI Group (UK) Ltd, Croydon, CR0 4YY
C9781394338597_031025

To my partner in work, life, and love—R. Trent Thompson— thank you for believing in this project from the beginning. Without your steady encouragement, this book would still be a thought bubble floating above my head.

To my children, Callie and Riley, my son-in-law, Jacob, and my grandchildren, Hudson and Grady—thank you for your patience and love, especially during Sunday brunches and playdates that were sometimes cut short in the service of a deadline. And to Kennedy, the original writer in our family, thank you for cheering me on and offering encouragement exactly when I needed it most.

And finally, I dedicate this book to fundraisers, nonprofit champions, and community leaders everywhere—your courage and commitment remind me daily of the power of collective action and our shared calling to make the world more just, more generous, and more joyful.

Contents

Foreword ix

Introduction xi

PART I Foundations and Evolution of Fundraising 1

Chapter 1 The Evolution of Fundraising: How We Got Here 3

Chapter 2 Navigating Donor-Centered Fundraising: Principles, Challenges, and Ethical Considerations 15

Chapter 3 Community-Centered Fundraising: Reimagining Philanthropy for Equity and Justice 31

Chapter 4 The Need for a New Approach: Human-Centered Fundraising 51

PART II Human-Centered Fundraising in Practice 67

Chapter 5 Assembling the Heroes: Building a Diverse Fundraising Team 69

Chapter 6 The League of Heroes Paradigm: Unity in Diversity 89

Chapter 7 Crafting the Narrative: Storytelling in Human-Centered Fundraising 113

Chapter 8 Navigating Power Dynamics in Human-Centered Fundraising 131

Contents

Chapter 9	The Hero's Journey: Implementing the Human-Centered Model	141
Chapter 10	AI: The Responsible and Beneficial Sidekick in Human-Centered Fundraising	165

PART III Challenges, Measurement, and the Future 189

Chapter 11	Navigating the Challenges: Overcoming Resistance to Change	191
Chapter 12	Measuring Impact: Metrics for a New Era of Fundraising	203
Chapter 13	The Future of Fundraising: Trends and Predictions	221

References	*241*
Bibliography	*243*
Acknowledgments	*245*
About the Author	*247*
Index	*249*

Foreword

When I met Tammy Zonker about five years ago, we connected instantly on a personal level. She lives in Detroit, a city close to my heart, as I spent my summers there with family. Our shared appreciation and deep affection for Detroit made our conversations especially meaningful.

Beyond that, Tammy is an exceptional fundraising professional, highly knowledgeable, credible, and widely respected. She is also a phenomenal teacher—engaging, insightful, and an absolute joy to learn from. With nearly 40 years in the fundraising profession, I know there is always more to learn, and Tammy is someone I truly enjoy learning from.

So, when she told me she had written a book, I was so excited and wanted a copy immediately. I knew it would be filled with invaluable insights and practical wisdom—and it did not disappoint. Tammy's gift for sharing knowledge and storytelling, so evident in her teaching and speaking, shines through on every page.

Every chapter offers something exceptional, but one that particularly stood out to me is Chapter 7. Tammy has a rare ability to forge an emotional connection between donors, nonprofits, and—most importantly—the communities being served. She demonstrates how compelling storytelling can bridge the gap between donor-centric and community-centric fundraising, making it one of the most powerful tools in a fundraiser's toolkit.

This book is a must-read for anyone in the nonprofit world. Tammy is exactly the right person to deliver these lessons, and you'll find just what you need within these pages. Enjoy!

—Birgit Burton
Founder and CEO of the African American Development Officers
Network & Immediate Past Chair of the Association of Fundraising
Professionals Global Board

Introduction

Throughout this book we'll discuss the intersection of donor-centered fundraising *(focused largely on people who hold the majority of wealth)* and community-centered fundraising *(focused on race, equity, and social justice)*. We'll navigate sensitive topics such as power dynamics, diversity, equity, and inclusion.

I recognize that I hold unearned privileges as a white, cisgendered woman. These privileges are not something I have earned or chosen; they are bestowed upon me by structures that favor individuals with my racial and gender identity. I understand that these privileges are not solely mine to enjoy but also part of a broader system perpetuating inequality. I commit to using my privilege to amplify the voices of marginalized people and work toward dismantling oppression systems. This includes listening to and believing the experiences of others, educating myself on issues of racial and gender justice, and advocating for policies and practices that promote equity and inclusion. I've been blessed by mentors and friends who have shared their experiences and insights as people of other races, faiths, and gender identities. They've generously schooled me on issues of social justice inequities and given me a safe space to ask questions. I am, and always will be, a grateful and humbled student.

Acknowledging my privilege is only the first step. I am committed to ongoing self-reflection and action to ensure that my privilege does not silence or overshadow the experiences of others but rather be a catalyst for positive change alongside you and others. With that understanding and your grace, let's get started!

Let me take you back to a pivotal moment in my nonprofit career journey during the throes of the US Great Recession in 2008. I was living in Indiana, working for a West Coast training company, crisscrossing the country, leading seminars and conferences, and teaching fundraising strategies. But it felt like we were stuck in a rut. The model we were using, deeply rooted in traditional fundraising strategies and best practices, was rigid, left little room for innovation, and wasn't producing the expected results in an increasingly difficult economy. My clients were struggling and looking to me for new ideas and solutions to their fundraising challenges.

That's when I realized what I needed—a fundraising sandbox, a space where experimentation and bold ideas could be tested, take root, and flourish. Detroit, with its resilience in the midst of adversity, stood out as the perfect crucible for transformation. So, I packed some things and set up a modest home-away-from-home in Motown in October 2008. I had just become an empty nester, so what was to stop me?

Detroit was hard hit by the Great Recession—a city grappling with the full force of the economic downturn where challenges seemingly loomed at every corner. Unemployment was 30%. Two of the three largest employers were in bankruptcy. The population had dropped from nearly three million to less than one million. One in five homes was in foreclosure. The City of Detroit was $18 billion in debt, with creditors circling. The only thing bigger than Detroit's challenges was the heart and determination of its people.

But, where some might have seen obstacles, I saw opportunities—a chance to create something truly transformative. I knew if I could successfully raise money in Detroit, I could raise money almost anywhere. Detroit became my fundraising laboratory, where I dared to experiment, learn, and push the boundaries of conventional fundraising wisdom.

After creating and testing, failing, iterating, and refining key strategies, I applied what I was learning from my Detroit fundraising experience and spearheaded the team effort that secured monumental gifts, like the $27.1 million from General Motors Foundation to United Way for Southeastern Michigan. I witnessed firsthand the transformative power of an inspiring CEO and Board vision, coupled with innovative programs and tailored fundraising strategies, when they engage passionate, community-focused individual and institutional partners.

Transforming the Children's Center

The Children's Center, a beacon of hope in Detroit, faced daunting hurdles. Their fundraising efforts were faltering, leaving critical programs underfunded. However, within these challenges lay opportunities for growth and impact.

By embracing bold, data-driven, tested, and proven strategies, we charted a new course. While the executive team and board were at first apprehensive about a plan loaded with innovative ideas and big, hairy, audacious goals, we rallied leadership and board members around a shared vision, revamped donor communications, and overhauled outdated systems. We also created a high-performing development team to help drive our mission forward and achieve our ambitious fundraising goals. We diversified funding streams beyond an events strategy. The result? A staggering tripling of philanthropy within the first three years and doubling it again six years later.

But it wasn't just about the numbers. It was about the people—the children and families who relied on organizations like The Children's Center to walk alongside them, often in their darkest moments. Their stories of determination and courage fueled my passion for creating change.

I'm sharing my journey with you because I firmly believe in John F. Kennedy's ideal that *"a high tide lifts all boats."* I believe there's an urgent need for fundraisers and nonprofit leaders everywhere to work together toward a transformed and sustainable future. I knew that if I could learn how to raise money successfully in Detroit during a catastrophic economic recession, then I could teach others how to raise money in the most difficult of circumstances.

My life's mission is to equip and empower fundraisers and nonprofit leaders like you to reach new heights of fundraising success. I believe in the power of collaboration and collective growth. It's my obsession.

United for the Greater Good

But here's my concern. Our world feels deeply divided, like everyone is taking sides on every little thing. The nonprofit sector has always been about bringing people together, about finding common ground, and working hand-in-hand to make a real difference.

Aren't we the helpers, peacemakers, the conveners, and the champions for goodness, comfort and healing, equity, inclusion, and possibilities? The ones who believe in a brighter tomorrow? Aren't we stronger when we work together? So why are we letting this debate over donor-centered versus community-centered fundraising divide us? What's this division costing us as a sector and those we serve? Our strength lies in our ability to unite, put aside our differences, find common ground, and focus on the greater good.

At the end of the day, I believe most of us want the same thing—to create positive change and build a better world for everyone. And we can't do that if we're too busy debating among ourselves. Every minute spent focusing on what separates us is a minute we could have spent working together to solve the problems our communities are facing. Do we have the will to find enough common ground and shared values to work together? I believe human-centered fundraising can help unite us in nearly every circumstance, with one exception:

As author and LGBTQ+ Activist, James Baldwin said, *"We can disagree and still love each other, unless your disagreement is rooted in my oppression and denial of my humanity and right to exist."*

What You Can Expect from This Book

The nonprofit sector is at a crossroads. We're letting debates over fundraising approaches divide us. I wrote this book to serve as a guide to implementing a human-centered approach to fundraising that combines the best of donor-centered and community-centered models. To help us all raise even more money and accelerate short and long-term goals while ensuring everyone has a seat at the table. With the proven strategies and tools that I share in this book, I'm fully committed to being a guide and partner in achieving our ambitious fundraising goals so we can create a brighter future for our communities and our sector.

This Human-Centered approach to fundraising stands on the broad shoulders of Donor-Centered Fundraising and Community-Centered Fundraising. For that, I'm deeply grateful for Penelope Burk and Vu Le, who birthed these movements and all those who have embraced, implemented, failed, learned, and iterated these diverse approaches.

My fondest dream is that Human-Centered Fundraising reflects the strengths of both approaches, mitigates the shadow side, and is embraced by you—fundraising professionals and nonprofit leaders everywhere. That you embody, learn, fail, iterate, and evolve this approach. I'll just say we won't perfect it. Because perfection means we stop getting better.

It Will Take You, Me—Everyone

I know we won't see eye-to-eye on everything—that's just life. But can't we find a way to come together despite our differences? Can we remember the values that brought us to this work in the first place—compassion, empathy, a commitment to justice, equitable access to education, healthcare, the arts, and more?

There's so much healing that needs to happen, so many wrongs that need to be made right. And the nonprofit sector has an important role to play in all of that. But we can only do it if we stand together, united in our approach and shared purpose.

So, let's take a deep breath, step back from the things that divide us, and remember what really matters. Let's get back to the work of bringing light to the darkness, of reaching out to those who have been pushed down for far too long. Because at the end of the day, that's what it's all about, isn't it? Mobilizing community toward making the world better than we found it.

The problems we fundraisers and nonprofit leaders aim to tackle are just too massive and complex for any single hero. Together, using a human-centered approach to fundraising, we can create a future where nonprofits thrive, where missions are fully funded, and where communities have the support they need to flourish. I invite you to join me on this journey of transformation. I can't do it alone. You can't do it alone. It will take all of us, heroes.

Reclaiming the Word "Hero"

For many, the word *hero* has become entangled with saviorism. I understand why—historically and systemically, it has sometimes created division and caused harm, perpetuating racism, classism, sexism, and ableism.

But that's not the hero I believe in.

As a kid growing up in the 1970s, I was glued to the *Wonder Woman* TV series starring Lynda Carter. I admired her brilliance, moral clarity, physical strength—and most of all, her unwavering commitment to goodness in action. She flew an invisible jet, deflected bullets with her bracelets, and wielded a golden lasso of truth … I mean, come on!

To me—and to generations of women and girls—she was a hero and an icon of feminist strength. But what made her even more powerful was her humility. She lived her life as Diana Prince, a government agent, quietly doing her job until the moment came to rise. Maybe your hero wasn't Wonder Woman. Maybe it was Black Panther, the Green Hornet, or someone else entirely. But I bet you felt the same tug toward courage, justice, and possibility.

That's why I believe it's time we reclaim the word *hero*.

By definition, a hero is someone admired for their courage, noble qualities, and outstanding achievements. Their traits?

- **Courage:** Facing fear, danger, or adversity head-on.
- **Selflessness:** Acting for the good of others, not personal gain.
- **Integrity:** Holding fast to values—even under pressure.
- **Inspiration:** Motivating others by example.
- **Fairness:** Treating people equitably—based on their needs, context, or contributions—while ensuring justice, honesty, and impartiality.

In my nearly 30 years as a fundraiser and nonprofit leader, I've met countless everyday heroes who embody those traits.

Like the Gunter family, who donated their Disney vacation savings so Detroit students could access remote learning during the pandemic. Or Ms. Christine, who volunteered over 1,000 hours in just one year—because she was deeply grateful for the care her daughters received at The Children's Center. Or Porsha, a scholarship recipient and first-generation college student who became the guardian of her young step-siblings after their parents were killed in a tragic accident. And the countless colleagues whose brilliance is matched only by their passion and purpose.

Each of us has the capacity to be an everyday hero. But just like the *Justice League*™ and *Avengers*™, our greatest strength is in coming together.

When we unite—bringing our gifts, lived experiences, and perspectives to the table—we create lasting change. We save lives. We build stronger communities.

So when I say *Calling All Heroes*, it's not a slogan—it's a rallying cry. It's a call for transformational leaders to rise. For donors to lead with generosity. For communities to lead with wisdom. And for all of us to lead with courage and heart.

Let's do this—together, Heroes!

Foundations and Evolution of Fundraising

Part I introduces you to the history, core philosophies, and evolving models of fundraising, setting the stage for a new, blended approach.

1 | The Evolution of Fundraising: How We Got Here

"Look back to learn how to look forward."
—Joe Girard, "World's Greatest Salesman,"
Motivational Speaker, and Author

Fundraising today stands at a pivotal intersection between donor-centered and community-centered approaches. For nonprofit leaders and fundraisers, this moment invites reflection: *How did we get here?* The journey from traditional methods to nuanced strategies has been shaped by historical, technological, and societal shifts. Before diving into these modern approaches, it's crucial to understand the roots of fundraising and the lessons they offer for navigating today's challenges.

The Early Days: Agency-Centered Fundraising

In the early years of nonprofit fundraising, the focus was agency-centered and transactional. Organizations communicated their needs with appeals like,

"We do this. We need that. Aren't we great? Please give!" While donors responded, the relationship rarely extended beyond a thank-you letter. The emphasis was on the organization's goals rather than the donor's motivations or values.

This approach mirrored practices in the for-profit sector during the 1960s, when businesses began exploring *customer-centricity*. Influential thinkers like Peter Drucker championed this concept, emphasizing that businesses succeed by understanding and meeting customer needs. Drucker famously stated, *"The purpose of business is to create and keep a customer,"* highlighting the importance of relationships over transactions.

As digital technologies emerged in the 1990s, businesses began using data to personalize customer experiences—a shift that nonprofits would later adopt. These developments laid the groundwork for more sophisticated fundraising strategies focused on building deeper connections with supporters.

The Historical Tides: How We Got Here

Let's journey back to the late 1980s. Under US President Ronald Reagan, nonprofits faced significant challenges due to substantial reductions in federal spending on social welfare programs. These cuts were dramatic, with federal spending on social welfare declining from $106.1 billion under President Jimmy Carter in fiscal year 1980 to $78.4 billion near the end of Reagan's presidency in fiscal year 1988. The only exceptions to these reductions were health and income assistance programs, which remained relatively intact.

As a result, the nonprofit sector experienced a transformative period that would reshape the fundraising landscape for decades to come. As government funding receded, private philanthropy emerged as the new lifeline for organizations seeking to make a difference. This shift marked the beginning of a competitive era in fundraising, where nonprofits had to innovate and differentiate themselves to attract private donors.

According to *Giving USA*, over the last 40 years, total giving in current dollars grew most significantly during the 10-year period from 1994 to 2003. Total giving increased by an impressive 97.8% during this time—59.4% when adjusted for inflation. This surge highlighted a growing reliance on private philanthropy as nonprofits adapted to meet donor expectations and secure sustainable funding.

As nonprofits adapted to the competitive fundraising landscape of the late 20th century, they were increasingly driven to innovate and refine their strategies to meet evolving donor expectations. This transformative period gave rise to groundbreaking philosophies, such as relationship fundraising, and set the stage for the emergence of donor-centered and community-centered approaches that continue to shape the sector today (see Figure 1.1).

Setting the Stage for Modern Fundraising Philosophies

Picture a vibrant, bustling marketplace of ideas and causes, with nonprofits of all shapes and sizes setting up shop. Each organization was eager to showcase its unique impact and value proposition, creating an environment reminiscent of a lively bazaar. Meanwhile, donors were undergoing their own

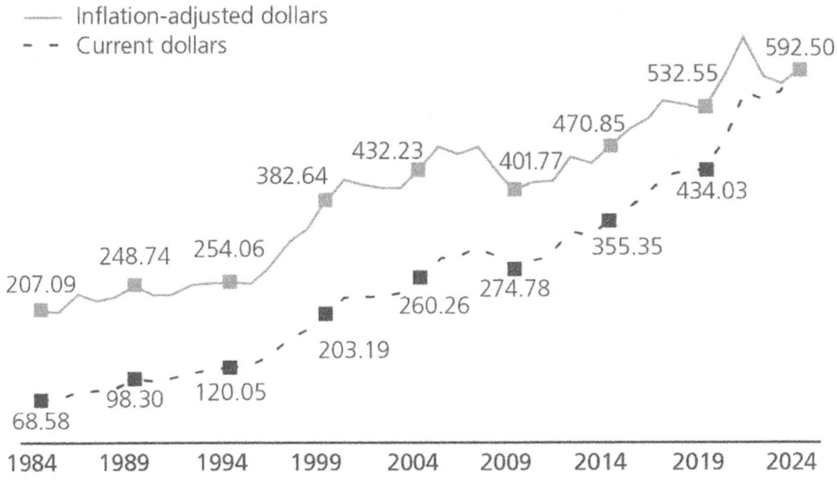

Figure 1.1   Trends in total giving, 1983–2024.

Source: Giving USA 2024/Giving USA Foundation.

evolution. The dawn of the information age ushered in unprecedented transparency, breaking down traditional barriers between givers and recipients.

Nonprofits began embracing digital technologies in the mid-1990s, with websites becoming essential tools for outreach and online giving by the early 2000s. Early adopters like Impact Online paved the way for innovations in online fundraising and volunteer engagement. In 1994, Greenpeace International embedded the first "Donate Now" button on its website. By 2008, features such as e-newsletters and "Donate Now" buttons had become standard elements of nonprofit digital strategies.

Charity watchdog organizations, such as CharityWatch (founded in 1992), Charity Navigator (2001), GuideStar (1994), and the BBB Wise Giving Alliance (2001), have profoundly reshaped donor expectations and nonprofit practices by emphasizing transparency, accountability, and measurable impact. These evaluators emerged in response to growing donor demand for clarity on how their contributions were being used. By providing accessible ratings based on financial health, governance, and program outcomes, watchdogs empower donors to make informed decisions while holding nonprofits accountable for their operations.

One of the most influential watchdogs, Charity Navigator, has played a pivotal role in shaping donor behavior since its founding in 2001. Its star rating system evaluates charities on financial health, accountability, transparency, and increasingly on impact metrics. Studies show that an increase in a charity's rating from three to four stars can lead to a 6–12% rise in donations, particularly for larger organizations with robust operational structures. These ratings have become a critical tool for nonprofits seeking to enhance their credibility and attract new donors.

The ripple effects of these ratings extend beyond donor behavior. Nonprofits often adjust their strategies to align with watchdog criteria. For example, some organizations focus on reducing administrative costs or improving governance structures to secure higher ratings. However, this emphasis can sometimes lead to unintended consequences, such as misreporting expenses or prioritizing easily measurable outcomes over long-term impact.

Charity Navigator's expansion into areas like leadership and culture evaluation has further influenced nonprofit practices. Its Encompass Rating System now includes indicators such as diversity, equity, inclusion (DEI), and constituent feedback mechanisms. This broader approach encourages nonprofits to adopt more holistic strategies while addressing donor concerns about ethical practices and social responsibility.

The impact of these watchdogs is evident in real-world examples. Organizations with high ratings often experience increased donations and visibility. For instance, White Pony Express leveraged its four-star rating to attract first-time donors from across the United States, significantly boosting its fundraising outcomes. Conversely, nonprofits with lower ratings may struggle to maintain donor trust and face challenges in securing funding.

By fostering a culture of transparency and accountability, charity watchdogs have transformed the nonprofit sector into a more data-driven and results-oriented space. While their influence is not without challenges—such as the potential for gaming the system—their role remains essential in building trust between donors and nonprofits. For fundraisers and nonprofit leaders, understanding these dynamics is critical for navigating today's philanthropic landscape effectively.

Relationship Fundraising: A Turning Point

Before donor-centered fundraising gained prominence through Penelope Burk's work in 2003, my dear friend Ken Burnett introduced *relationship fundraising* in 1992. This groundbreaking approach emphasized building strong, lifelong connections between nonprofits and their supporters by treating donors as valued partners rather than mere contributors. Burnett's philosophy centered on understanding donors' motivations and creating mutually beneficial relationships that prioritize trust, satisfaction, and commitment.

Burnett's concept of relationship fundraising evolved from his earlier work in the 1990s, where he introduced the idea of building *"Friends for life"* through respectful donor-centric practices. His book *Relationship Fundraising*, now in its third edition, has expanded to include essential elements such as personalization, appreciation, and effective communication. These principles are designed to foster deeper connections between donors and the causes they support while enhancing fundraising outcomes.

As a fundraiser since 1977, Burnett saw relationship fundraising as a strategic shift from transactional methods to a more holistic approach.

By focusing on donors' emotional and psychological needs—such as identity, well-being, and love—Burnett's methods have proven to be transformative for nonprofits seeking to build lasting donor relationships. His work has laid the foundation for modern donor-centric practices while continuing to influence the sector's evolution.

Key Elements of Ken Burnett's Relationship Fundraising

- **Donor-Centric Approach:** Fundraisers should prioritize understanding donors' motivations and values, treating them as shareholders in the mission rather than mere customers.
- **Personalization and Appreciation:** Communication with donors should be tailored to their preferences and include genuine expressions of gratitude.
- **Effective Communication:** Storytelling and clear messaging are vital for inspiring action and maintaining engagement.
- **Beyond Transactions:** The focus should be on nurturing long-term relationships that lead to sustained support rather than one-time gifts.
- **Adaptation to New Technologies:** While leveraging digital tools is essential, the core principles of relationship fundraising remain rooted in personal connections.

The Evolution of Relationship Fundraising

Over time, Burnett's vision has expanded to incorporate new strategies and technologies while remaining true to its core philosophy of integrity, honesty, and frequent feedback. The third edition of *Relationship Fundraising* delves deeper into the psychological needs of donors, influenced by the work of Dr. Adrian Sargeant and Dr. Jen Shang at the Institute for Sustainable Philanthropy in the United Kingdom.

Burnett's contributions have profoundly shaped how nonprofits approach donor engagement. His emphasis on meaningful relationships continues to inspire fundraisers worldwide as they strive to create sustainable models that balance organizational goals with donor satisfaction.

Connecting Burnett's Principles to Modern Donor-Centered Practices

In today's digital era, Burnett's principles serve as a timeless foundation for innovative donor-centered practices that leverage technology without losing the human touch. By integrating his strategies with modern tools like AI segmentation and personalized campaigns, nonprofits can achieve both enhanced fundraising outcomes and deeper emotional connections with their supporters—laying the groundwork for sustainable growth and impact.

For instance, nonprofits now use advanced tools like predictive analytics and AI-powered platforms to understand donor behaviors and motivations at a granular level. These technologies allow fundraisers to segment donors based on giving patterns, event-driven motivations, or lapsed engagement, creating tailored outreach strategies that resonate deeply with individual supporters. Burnett's focus on personalization finds new life in these approaches, ensuring that each donor feels valued and understood.

Take the example of personalized digital campaigns. Today's donors expect nonprofits to engage with them as individuals rather than generic contributors. Platforms like Classy Studio enable organizations to craft branded donation pages that mirror campaign messaging across email, social media, and direct mail. These cohesive experiences not only reinforce trust but also drive higher conversion rates and retention. Burnett's principle of effective communication—through storytelling and clear messaging—is amplified in these digital-first strategies, where every interaction is designed to inspire action and deepen connection.

AI-driven tools further enhance Burnett's vision by enabling nonprofits to anticipate donor needs and preferences. For example, AI can identify recurring donors with increased financial capacity or flag lapsed donors for re-engagement campaigns. These insights allow fundraisers to approach donors with tailored asks or personalized messages that align with their giving history and interests—transforming the transactional nature of fundraising into a meaningful partnership.

Burnett's emphasis on nurturing long-term relationships over one-time transactions also resonates with the growing trend of monthly giving programs. By offering donors convenient ways to contribute regularly, non-profits can build sustained support while fostering a sense of community around their mission. This approach echoes Burnett's philosophy of creating "Friends for life," ensuring that donors remain engaged and invested in the cause over time.

Case Studies: Applying Relationship Fundraising Principles

Ken Burnett's principles have been successfully applied across diverse organizations, demonstrating their adaptability and impact:

Botton Village (Camphill Village Trust)   In the early 1980s, Burnett collaborated with Botton Village to implement monthly giving and legacy giving programs. This strategy resulted in exceptional success, with legacy income estimated between £100 million and £180 million over several decades.

- **Key Success Factors:** Long-term donor relationships built on personalized engagement fostered loyalty.
- **Broader Trends:** Monthly giving aligns with modern donor preferences for predictable contributions, while legacy giving reflects the growing importance of sustainability in nonprofit funding.
- **Scalability:** Smaller organizations can replicate this model by using online tools for monthly giving campaigns or hosting workshops on legacy planning.

National Youth Orchestra of the UK   Burnett helped establish a sustainable donor base for the National Youth Orchestra by prioritizing regular donations and legacy gifts.

- **Key Success Factors:** Focusing on donor experience led to consistent support.
- **Broader Trends:** Regular donations reflect donors' preference for ongoing engagement with causes they care about.
- **Scalability:** Community arts groups can adapt these strategies through intimate events or exclusive perks for donors.

ActionAid Burnett transformed ActionAid into one of the UK's top charities by emphasizing monthly giving as a cornerstone of relationship fundraising.

- **Key Success Factors:** Lifelong donor relationships resulted in substantial growth.
- **Broader Trends:** Monthly giving appeals to donors seeking convenience and connection with causes.
- **Scalability:** Nonprofits can use storytelling campaigns or partner with local advisors to promote legacy gifts effectively.

These case studies illustrate how relationship fundraising principles can be scaled across various sectors while highlighting broader trends in modern philanthropy. By adopting these strategies, nonprofits can build stronger donor relationships that ensure financial sustainability and deepen their impact over time.

Modern Approaches: Donor-Centered vs. Community-Centered Fundraising

While relationship fundraising laid the foundation for donor-centered practices, community-centered fundraising has emerged as an alternative that prioritizes collective impact over individual contributions. Both approaches offer valuable lessons:

- **Donor-Centered Fundraising** focuses on understanding individual motivations and tailoring engagement strategies.
- **Community-Centered Fundraising** emphasizes inclusivity and shared responsibility for addressing societal challenges.

Fundraisers must critically evaluate these models to create hybrid strategies that balance individual relationships with broader community goals.

Key Takeaways and Action Steps

Key Takeaways

- **Understand Historical Context:** Recognize how shifts in funding sources and donor expectations have shaped modern fundraising practices.
- **Prioritize Relationships Over Transactions:** Build meaningful connections with donors through personalization, appreciation, and effective communication.
- **Leverage Technology Thoughtfully:** Use digital tools to enhance engagement while maintaining authenticity.
- **Adapt Proven Strategies:** Learn from successful case studies to scale relationship-focused approaches within your organization.
- **Balance Donor-Centered and Community-Centered Goals:** Create strategies that honor individual contributions while fostering collective impact.

Action Steps

- Conduct a donor survey to understand motivations and preferences.
- Implement monthly giving programs using accessible online platforms.
- Develop storytelling campaigns that connect emotionally with supporters.
- Host workshops or events promoting legacy giving tailored to your community.
- Evaluate your organization's transparency using tools like GuideStar or Charity Navigator.

By embracing these principles, fundraisers can navigate today's challenges with confidence while building a sustainable future for their organizations and communities.

Bridging the Past and Future of Fundraising

As we reflect on the evolution of fundraising—from agency-centered beginnings to the emergence of relationship fundraising—it becomes clear that the nonprofit sector has continually adapted to meet the shifting needs of donors and communities. These transformations have laid the groundwork for today's approaches, where fundraisers must navigate the delicate balance between engaging individual donors and addressing collective community goals.

In the next few chapters, we'll delve deeper into this dynamic interplay by exploring the origins and evolution, core principles, strengths, and challenges of donor-centered and community-centered fundraising. Together, we'll examine how these approaches shape the way nonprofits connect with supporters, inspire action, and drive meaningful change—and how combining their best elements can lead to a more holistic, impactful strategy.

2 | Navigating Donor-Centered Fundraising: Principles, Challenges, and Ethical Considerations

"What good is an idea if it remains an idea? Try. Experiment. Iterate. Fail. Try again. Change the world."

—Simon Sinek, American Author, Inspirational Speaker, and Leadership Expert

Imagine yourself at the helm of a nonprofit organization, steering through the unpredictable waters of fundraising. On one side, you glimpse the polished shores of donor-centered fundraising, offering promises of abundant resources and loyal supporters. On the other side, you see the vibrant terrain of community-centered fundraising rooted in equity and collective impact. Which course do you chart? If you're like most nonprofit leaders, you've likely felt torn between these two approaches, unsure which path will best serve your mission. Trust me— I've been there.

The Origins and Evolution of Donor-Centered Fundraising

Let's take a journey back to the late 1990s and early 2000s—the era when donor-centered fundraising (DCF) began reshaping nonprofit strategies. Pioneers like Ken Burnett and Penelope Burk revolutionized the field by emphasizing the importance of treating donors as individuals rather than mere financial contributors. Burk's work especially highlighted the importance of understanding donor motivations and building authentic relationships, which led to the widespread adoption of DCF as a best practice in the nonprofit sector.

Penelope Burk's groundbreaking research revealed that understanding donor motivations was akin to discovering a new continent in the nonprofit world. Her work underscored three key principles:

- Acknowledging contributions promptly and meaningfully
- Communicating the tangible impact of donations before soliciting further gifts
- Fostering genuine, personal relationships with donors

This data-driven approach gained traction, inspiring nonprofits to prioritize donor engagement as a cornerstone of their fundraising strategies.

Core Principles of Donor-Centered Fundraising

At its heart, donor-centered fundraising is about building authentic connections with donors by understanding their motivations, interests, and values. Think of it as tending to a garden: each donor is a unique plant requiring personalized care to thrive. Here are some foundational elements:

- **Prompt and Meaningful Acknowledgment**
  Donors should receive timely and personalized recognition for their contributions. This could include heartfelt thank-you letters, phone calls, or even small tokens of appreciation. Research shows that prompt acknowledgment not only makes donors feel appreciated but also increases the likelihood of future gifts.

- **Transparency and Accountability**
  Organizations must clearly communicate how donations are used. By assigning each gift to a specific program or initiative, non-profits can show donors the tangible impact of their contributions, reinforcing trust and loyalty.

- **Impact Reporting**
  Before asking for another gift, it's essential to provide measurable reports on what previous contributions have accomplished. This practice builds credibility and demonstrates that donations are making a meaningful difference.

- **Personalized Engagement**
  Tailoring communication to align with each donor's unique interests and motivations helps foster deeper connections. Whether through tailored updates or invitations to relevant events, personalization ensures donors feel understood and valued.

- **Managing Expectations**
  Clearly outline what donors can expect in return for their support. Avoid over-solicitation or focusing solely on financial asks, as these practices can alienate donors over time.

- **Stewardship**
  Responsible management of funds is critical to maintaining donor trust. This includes ensuring donations are used effectively and efficiently to achieve intended goals.

- **Prioritizing Donor Satisfaction**
  Penelope Burk's research highlights the transformative impact of prioritizing donor satisfaction on retention rates and gift sizes. For instance, donor-centered fundraising achieves a 67% renewal rate

compared to 35% in traditional approaches. Additionally, 52% of donors are more likely to make larger gifts when they renew.

By implementing these principles, nonprofits can create a sustainable fundraising model that not only retains donors but also inspires them to increase their support over time.

How DCF Principles Apply Across Donor Types and Organizational Contexts

While these principles are universal, their application varies:

- **Major Donors:** Require highly personalized engagement, in-depth reporting, and cultivation over time. Moves management strategies are commonly used here.
- **Recurring Donors:** Value regular updates and recognition; ongoing stewardship and community-building opportunities are effective.
- **Corporate Donors:** Seek alignment with their brand and public recognition; impact stories and partnership opportunities are key.
- **Foundations:** Require detailed reporting and evidence of impact; stewardship is often formalized through grant management.
- **Small Grassroots Nonprofits:** May struggle to provide highly personalized experiences due to limited resources but can excel at authentic, mission-driven engagement and community-building.
- **Large Established Nonprofits:** Often have systems for sophisticated segmentation and stewardship but must guard against depersonalization and mission drift.

Research-Based Benefits of Donor-Centered Fundraising

Research indicates that implementing donor-centered fundraising principles can have a significant positive impact on nonprofit organizations. Key findings include:

- **Enhanced Donor Engagement and Loyalty:** Donor-centered approaches prioritize building genuine relationships through personalized communication and recognizing donor contributions, which increase loyalty and retention rates (Sargeant & Jay, 2015).

- **Increased Giving and Support:** Organizations that adopt donor-centric practices often see higher donation levels, as donors feel valued and understood, leading to increased trust and willingness to give repeatedly (Bishop & Greenfield, 2018).
- **Improved Organizational Sustainability:** By fostering long-term donor relationships, nonprofits can secure consistent funding streams, reducing reliance on short-term campaigns and increasing resilience (James & Wymer, 2019).
- **Better Understanding of Donor Motivations:** A donor-centered approach encourages organizations to research and understand what motivates their supporters, enabling more effective stewardship and targeted appeals (Sargeant et al., 2020).
- **Positive Organizational Culture:** Emphasizing donor needs shifts organizational focus toward transparency and accountability, strengthening reputation and credibility in the community (Smith & Symonds, 2021a).

Most research supports that shifts toward donor-centered fundraising produce sustainable growth, improved organizational reputation, and stronger community trust.

Case Study: Prisma Health Upstate

Prisma Health Upstate, part of Prisma Health in Greenville, South Carolina, implemented a donor-centric approach by introducing gift planning early in their high-affinity, higher-capacity donors' cycle of generosity. This strategy focused on understanding and aligning with the donors' values and motivations.

- **Donor-Centric Gift Planning:** Prisma Health Upstate's Office of Philanthropy made a deliberate decision to engage donors early in their cycle of generosity. This involved personalized communication and planning tailored to each donor's interests and capacity.

- **Increased Current Giving:** Once donors added charitable beneficiaries to their estate plans, their current giving increased significantly. On average, donations rose by 77% over a four-year period compared to the previous four years, from $4,355 to $7,699 annually.
- **Long-Term Engagement:** By engaging donors early and deeply, Prisma Health Upstate ensured that these donors would remain involved for decades, fostering a long-term relationship that went beyond financial contributions.

Benefits

- **Enhanced Donor Engagement:** Donors felt valued and involved, leading to deeper connections with the organization.
- **Increased Financial Support:** The strategy resulted in a substantial increase in annual donations.
- **Sustained Impact:** Donors experienced the joy of seeing the impact of their generosity during their lifetime, which motivated them to continue supporting the cause.

This case study demonstrates how a donor-centric approach can lead to increased engagement, financial support, and long-term commitment from donors, ultimately benefiting both the organization and the donors themselves.

Strengths vs. Challenges of Donor-Centered Fundraising

While DCF has proven effective for many nonprofits, it is not without its complexities. Donor-centered fundraising has proven to be an effective strategy for building strong relationships, increasing retention, and fostering donor loyalty. However, it also comes with inherent challenges that nonprofit leaders must navigate carefully. To better understand the nuances of donor-centered fundraising, let's look at its strengths and shadow side in Table 2.1.

These shadow sides often arise when organizations confuse being *donor-centric* with catering excessively to egocentric preferences—a distinction worth exploring further.

Table 2.1 Strengths and Shadow Side of Donor-Centered Fundraising

Strengths	Shadow Side
Increased Donor Retention: Strong relationships foster donor loyalty and long-term support.	**Power Imbalance:** Donors may exert undue influence over the organization's mission, leading to "mission drift."
Higher Donation Amounts: Effective engagement with major donors encourages generous giving.	**Perpetuation of Inequity:** Can reinforce a "savior complex" and marginalize beneficiaries.
Enhanced Donor Loyalty: Loyal donors become advocates, attracting new supporters and enhancing credibility.	**Ethical Concerns:** May prioritize donor needs over beneficiary dignity and rights, creating ethical dilemmas.
Improved Fundraising Effectiveness: Personalized communication and strategic allocation increase donor satisfaction.	**Organizational Challenges:** Overemphasis on external relationships can strain resources and lead to staff burnout.
Simplicity and Focus: Clear focus on donor engagement makes it easier to implement and maintain effective strategies.	**Lack of Honest Conversations:** This may oversimplify complex, systemic issues with donors and/or perpetuate stereotypes and cultural misconceptions.

It's important to note that these challenges often emerge when organizations confuse donor-centrism with catering to egocentric individuals. Fundraising expert and author Jim Langley emphasizes that truly donor-centric practices are about building strategic partnerships with donors who value community impact over personal recognition. Langley observes that organizations struggling to demonstrate meaningful results may be more likely to cater to egos out of necessity, underscoring the importance of aligning fundraising strategies with clear, measurable outcomes.

From personal experience as a fundraiser, I've seen how tempting it can be to agree with a donor's misconceptions about the people served by our programs or their oversimplified solutions to complex problems. At first glance, this may seem like the path of least resistance. But at what cost? When we cave to this inclination, we do a disservice not only to those we serve but also to our organizations and even the donors themselves.

Donor-centered fundraising was never intended to cater to donors' off-mission ideas or preferences. Instead, it is meant to foster authentic partnerships rooted in shared values and mutual respect. By maintaining this focus, nonprofits can avoid mission drift while ensuring their work remains impactful and aligned with their core purpose.

Understanding donor motivations and maintaining ongoing communication not only boosts financial support but also contributes to organizational stability. Aligning fundraising strategies with donors' motivations such as altruism, social recognition, or personal values can strengthen donor relationships and improve fundraising outcomes.

Emphasizing the importance of adopting a donor-centric approach, research consistently shows that personalized communication and relationship management lead to increased donor loyalty and long-term support. Donor-centered strategies directly influence donor retention: organizations focusing on personalized engagement, acknowledgment, and relationship-building see significant improvements in donor loyalty and lifetime value.

Furthermore, organizations that foster a culture of transparency, accountability, and donor focus tend to develop stronger trust and support from their communities.

While donor-centered fundraising has driven significant success for many organizations, its limitations have sparked interest in alternative approaches that prioritize equity and shared decision-making—a topic we'll explore in depth in the next chapter.

Common Mistakes and Pitfalls in Donor-Centered Fundraising

While DCF is powerful, nonprofits often fall into these traps:

- **Overemphasizing Donor Preferences:** Leading to mission drift or diluted focus.
- **Neglecting Relationship Building:** Treating donors as ATMs rather than partners.
- **Asking Too Soon or Too Aggressively:** Damaging trust and turning donors off.
- **One-Size-Fits-All Communication:** Failing to segment and personalize for different donor types.
- **Overpromising Impact:** Creating unrealistic expectations and risking trust.
- **Failing to Educate Donors:** Not helping donors understand the broader context and systemic challenges.

Nonprofits should regularly review their practices to ensure they are building genuine, mission-aligned partnerships, not just maximizing short-term revenue.

Equity and Unintended Consequences of Donor-Centrism

Donor-centered fundraising, if unexamined, can unintentionally perpetuate inequity or exclusion:

- **Savior Complex:** Overemphasizing donors as "heroes" can reinforce harmful power dynamics and diminish the voices of those served when donors are recognized as the only "heroes."
- **Systemic Injustice:** Focusing on donor comfort can prevent honest conversations about privilege, race, and the root causes of inequity.
- **Exclusion of Marginalized Communities:** Traditional DCF often centers white, affluent donors, overlooking communities of color and the lived experience of those most impacted by the nonprofit's work.
- **Resource Disparities:** Small, minority-led nonprofits may struggle to meet donor expectations set by larger organizations, exacerbating inequity in the sector.
- **Transactional Charity:** Overly specific impact reporting can obscure the holistic, collective nature of nonprofit work and reinforce the "overhead myth."

The Ego Trap: A Word of Caution

As we dive deeper into donor-centered practices, it's crucial to distinguish between being donor-centric and catering to egocentrism. Langley emphasizes that true donor-centrism isn't about flattering wealthy individuals or providing exclusive access. Rather, it focuses on building trust, aligning shared values, and demonstrating measurable impact.

Langley argues that the vast majority of donors, including those with considerable wealth, give for altruistic reasons rather than ego gratification. He provides a helpful framework contrasting egocentric motivations with donor-centric practices, shown in Table 2.2.

Organizations must resist the temptation to prioritize ego-driven motivations over authentic partnerships that align with their mission.

Navigating Unintended Consequences

As DCF gained popularity, some nonprofits inadvertently shifted toward transactional practices focused on maintaining donor satisfaction at all costs, even when doing so conflicted with community needs or organizational values. This has led to concerns such as:

- **Mission Drift:** Organizations may add programs or initiatives solely to appease donors rather than staying true to their strategic goals.
- **Power Imbalances:** Wealthy donors might exert disproportionate influence over decisions, sidelining community voices.
- **Ethical Concerns:** Prioritizing donor preferences over beneficiary dignity can create moral dilemmas.

Table 2.2   Egocentric Motivations vs. Donor-Centric Practices

Egocentrism	Donor-Centrism
Seeks flattery	Seeks substantive interaction
Craves recognition	Cares about community ROI
Wants elite access	Wants access to changemakers
Loves profuse thanks	Loves making meaningful differences

To avoid these pitfalls, nonprofits must strike a balance between engaging donors effectively and serving communities equitably.

Fundraising expert Jim Langley reminds us that truly donor-centric practices focus on building strategic partnerships rather than catering to egocentric preferences. These partnerships emphasize shared impact and community ROI over personal recognition or exclusive access. However, organizations struggling to demonstrate meaningful results may find themselves tempted to prioritize donor egos out of necessity—a trap that can undermine their mission and values.

A distraught client once called me seeking advice about a situation that perfectly illustrates this dilemma. A friend of a major donor and trustee introduced a business acquaintance interested in funding a program at her organization. Initially, the opportunity seemed promising. The prospective donor couple, wealthy and seemingly philanthropic, owned several businesses both domestically and internationally. Over time, my client invested significant resources into cultivating the relationship: she gave them a campus tour, shared inspiring impact stories, and arranged meetings with her Executive Director to discuss the organization's strategic plan. At their request, she provided program outcomes reports, financial statements, and endowment performance data. The referring trustee even hosted the couple for dinner with executive leadership.

After months of effort, the prospective donors offered $500,000—but with a catch. They wanted to fund a named prison ministry program that was completely unrelated to the organization's mission and vision. My client felt deeply embarrassed in front of her Executive Director and Trustee. She was frustrated by the time and resources spent on building the relationship and felt deceived by their intentions. To make matters worse, the couple implied they would fund core programs even more generously if the organization agreed to bring their prison ministry program to life.

Ultimately, my client learned that staying true to their mission, even when it means declining substantial gifts, is critical for maintaining organizational integrity and community trust.

This experience highlights an important truth: donor-centered fundraising was never designed to cater to donors' off-mission ideas, no matter how well-intentioned they may seem. When nonprofits fear pushing back on donors, they risk acquiescing their own power and compromising their values. This dynamic is explored further in Chapter 8, "Navigating Power Dynamics in Human-Centered Fundraising."

This shift has sparked critical conversations about how nonprofits can balance donor satisfaction with community needs while striving for fundraising approaches that are both effective and equitable. It's akin to baking a cake that's both delicious and nutritious—a challenging but worthwhile endeavor that requires careful attention to ingredients and proportions. By staying true to their mission and fostering authentic partnerships, organizations can avoid falling into the ego trap while ensuring their work remains impactful and aligned with their values.

Technology: A Double-Edged Sword

As donor-centered fundraising gained popularity, technological advancements began to reshape the landscape. Early donor management systems evolved into sophisticated constituent relationship management (CRM) platforms capable of tracking donor preferences, automating key functions, analyzing giving patterns, and predicting future donor behavior. These tools have empowered nonprofits to streamline operations and engage donors more effectively. Digital communication channels have enabled personalized outreach at scale, while social media has created new opportunities for donor and volunteer recognition, as well as fostering community building.

These technological innovations have undoubtedly transformed fundraising, but they come with their own set of challenges. While technology has made personalization more achievable, it has sometimes reduced authentic human connection to automated journeys and algorithmic segmentation. It's like having a robot butler—efficient and precise but lacking the warmth and empathy of a human touch.

The most successful organizations have learned to use technology as an enabler of genuine relationships rather than a replacement for them. They understand that the goal isn't to automate empathy but to leverage tools that free up time for fundraisers to cultivate meaningful, personal interactions. For example, CRM systems can help fundraisers identify trends and tailor outreach strategies without losing sight of the human element.

Additionally, artificial intelligence (AI) is becoming a key player in the fundraising space. While AI offers exciting possibilities for predictive analytics and donor engagement, its ethical and beneficial use requires careful consideration. This topic will be explored further in Chapter 10, "AI: The Responsible and Beneficial Sidekick in Human-Centered Fundraising."

Reflection Point

Take a moment to think about your organization's major donor strategies. Do they emphasize impact and partnership or recognition and special access? Which approach is values-focused, and which is transactional-focused? How might this affect your mission over time?

While donor-centered fundraising has enabled many nonprofits to expand their impact, it has also sparked important conversations about balancing donor needs with community priorities. The key lies in finding that equilibrium where all stakeholders feel valued while keeping the organization's mission at the forefront.

Self-Reflection Questions

- **How does your organization currently approach major donor strategies?**

  Do they prioritize impact and partnership, or do they focus on recognition and special access? Reflect on whether your strategies align with your mission and values.

- **In what ways might a donor-first approach unintentionally sideline the voices and needs of the communities your organization serves?**

  Consider how prioritizing donor preferences might affect your ability to address systemic issues or amplify the voices of those with lived experiences related to your mission.

- **What steps can you take to balance the needs and expectations of donors with the priorities of the communities you aim to serve?**

  Identify actionable ways to ensure that donor engagement remains authentic and mission-driven while fostering equity and shared impact.

By reflecting on these questions, nonprofit leaders can better understand how their fundraising strategies shape their organization's long-term mission and community impact. Balancing donor satisfaction with community priorities is not only possible but essential for creating sustainable, equitable change.

Key Takeaways and Action Steps

Key Takeaways

- Donor-centered fundraising builds strong relationships but requires careful navigation to avoid ethical pitfalls.
- Balancing donor satisfaction with community priorities is essential for long-term success.
- Technology should enhance—not replace—human connection in fundraising efforts.

Action Steps

- Implement prompt acknowledgment practices that express genuine gratitude for every gift, regardless of gift amount.
- Develop transparent reporting systems that link donations directly to measurable outcomes.
- Engage donors through personalized communication tailored to their interests while keeping your mission central.
- Regularly evaluate your strategies for signs of mission drift or power imbalances.
- Use technology strategically—freeing up time for fundraisers to focus on authentic relationships rather than tasks and processes that can be automated.

By embracing these principles, nonprofit leaders can chart a course toward effective and equitable fundraising practices that honor both donors' generosity and communities' needs while staying true to their organizational missions.

From Donors to Communities: Expanding the Fundraising Lens

As we close this chapter on donor-centered fundraising, we've explored its transformative potential, nuanced challenges, and the delicate balance required to maintain alignment with organizational missions. Yet, as impactful as donor-centered strategies can be, they represent only one side of the fundraising coin.

The nonprofit sector is increasingly recognizing the need for approaches that prioritize equity and amplify community voices. Community-centered fundraising offers a compelling alternative—one that shifts the focus from individual donors to collective impact and shared responsibility. It's a model rooted in collaboration, justice, and the belief that those closest to the challenges are also closest to the solutions.

Interestingly, many of the challenges inherent in donor-centered fundraising—such as power imbalances, mission drift, and perpetuation of inequities—are directly addressed by community-centered practices. By focusing on equity and shared decision-making, community-centered fundraising seeks to empower nonprofits to build partnerships that reflect the voices and needs of those they serve.

In the next chapter, we'll dive into the origins and evolution of community-centered fundraising. We'll examine how this approach redefines philanthropy by centering communities as equal stakeholders in driving change. Get ready to explore a vision of fundraising that challenges traditional power dynamics and empowers nonprofits to build more inclusive and equitable futures.

3

Community-Centered Fundraising: Reimagining Philanthropy for Equity and Justice

"The community is best served if we see ourselves as part of a larger ecosystem working collectively to build a just society."
—Vu Le, Community-Centered Fundraising
Advocate, Speaker, Writer

On a rainy Thursday evening in San Francisco, the board and staff of a small arts nonprofit gathered for their annual fundraising strategy session. For years, their approach had been textbook: identify major donors, craft personalized appeals, and celebrate the generosity of their top supporters. But that night, something changed. A community member, let's call her Julia, a local artist and volunteer, stood up and asked, "How are we making sure our fundraising reflects the voices and needs of the people we serve?" The room fell silent. For the first time, the organization realized that fundraising could be more than a means to an end; it could be a tool for building trust, equity, and shared power within their community.

Julia's question echoes a growing movement across the nonprofit sector: the call for community-centered fundraising (CCF). This chapter explores the origins, principles, challenges, and future of CCF and how organizations like yours can blend its best elements with traditional practices for greater impact.

The Roots and Principles of Community-Centered Fundraising

Community-centered fundraising is not a brand-new concept. Its roots stretch back to mutual aid societies and grassroots movements led by Black, Indigenous, and People of Color (BIPOC) communities. These groups have long practiced collective giving and resource sharing as a means of survival and empowerment, often outside mainstream philanthropy.

Fundraising has always been about relationships—between nonprofits, donors, and the communities they serve. But what if we've been looking at those relationships through the wrong lens? Enter **community-centered fundraising (CCF)**, a transformative approach that shifts the focus from individual donors to the collective well-being of communities. If traditional donor-centered fundraising is like tending to individual plants, CCF is about nurturing an entire ecosystem. It's a bold reimagining of philanthropy that prioritizes equity, inclusivity, and shared power over charity models rooted in hierarchy and privilege.

A national study, *Adopting Community-Centric Fundraising: Findings from A National Study* (Dale and Hemachandra, 2025) was published by the Dorothy A. Johnson Center for Philanthropy at Grand Valley State University and the AFP Foundation for Philanthropy. This groundbreaking study surveyed 283 nonprofit organizations and conducted in-depth interviews with 14 fundraising professionals to assess the adoption of Community-Centric Fundraising practices across the US, noting that more organizations with knowledge and experience in CCF participated in the survey. It offered valuable insights into promising developments and persistent challenges in transforming established fundraising approaches. The study confirms that CCF, proposed in 2019 by leaders of color, is gaining significant traction as nonprofits seek to align fundraising with movements for race, equity, and social justice.

Why Community-Centered Fundraising?

CCF emerged from a growing awareness that conventional fundraising methods often perpetuate inequities rather than dismantling them. The 2008 financial crisis exposed deep economic disparities and raised critical questions about the effectiveness of traditional philanthropy. Advocates like Vu Le began asking: *Shouldn't our fundraising practices reflect the values we champion—equity, justice, and community empowerment?*

Advocates of the approach emphasize the importance of considering equity and social justice and addressing systemic challenges like racism and economic inequality in our fundraising work. Influential voices like Vu Le have been at the forefront of this movement, emphasizing the need to decolonize wealth and confront systemic inequities in philanthropy. Through his book *Unicorns on Fire*, his popular blog *Nonprofit AF*, and his public speaking engagements, Le has challenged the nonprofit sector to face uncomfortable truths about power imbalances inherent in traditional fundraising models.

While Vu Le is often credited with catalyzing the community-centered fundraising movement, he is quick to acknowledge that this work builds on decades of contributions by individuals and organizations that are frequently overlooked. The Community-Centric Fundraising (CCF) website highlights its debt to pioneers such as the Grassroots Institute for Fundraising Training, The People's Institute for Survival and Beyond, Non-Profit Anti-Racism Coalition, Social Justice Fund Northwest, Western States Center, and INCITE! Women of Color Against Violence. INCITE!'s seminal work, *The Revolution Will Not Be Funded: Beyond the Nonprofit Industrial Complex*, has been particularly influential in shaping critiques of traditional philanthropy. Additionally, thought leaders such as Angela Davis, Audre Lorde, Grace Lee Boggs, James Baldwin, and countless others have laid the intellectual foundation for this movement.

This collective legacy underscores a fundamental tenet of CCF: movements are never created by one individual but are instead the culmination of years of effort by many voices working toward a shared vision of equity and justice. By acknowledging these roots, CCF invites fundraisers to honor this history while forging new paths toward transformative change.

This approach challenges nonprofits to confront uncomfortable truths about systemic inequities embedded in philanthropy. It's not just about raising money; it's about rethinking how we build relationships with donors and communities to create lasting social change.

The Driving Principles of CCF

At its core, CCF is guided by 10 principles designed to foster collaboration, inclusivity, and equity in nonprofit work. These principles are a roadmap for fundraisers seeking to align their practices with social justice goals:

1. **Fundraising must be grounded in race, equity, and social justice**: This includes addressing systemic inequities and ensuring that fundraising practices promote fairness and inclusivity.
2. **Individual organizational missions are not as important as the collective community**: The focus is on the broader community's needs rather than individual organizational goals.
3. **Nonprofits are generous with and mutually supportive of one another**: Organizations collaborate instead of competing, working together to strengthen the community.
4. **All who engage in strengthening the community are equally valued**: Volunteers, staff, donors, and board members are all recognized as essential contributors.
5. **Time is valued equally as money**: Contributions of time and talent are treated with the same importance as financial donations.
6. **Donors are treated as partners**: This involves transparency, open communication, and sometimes difficult but necessary conversations about priorities and impact.
7. **Fostering a sense of belonging rather than othering**: Efforts are made to avoid exclusionary practices or stereotypes in fundraising approaches.

8. **Promoting understanding that everyone benefits from engaging in social justice work**: Fundraising is framed as a shared responsibility that benefits all participants, not just an act of charity.
9. **Viewing social justice work as holistic and transformative, not transactional**: The focus is on long-term systemic change rather than short-term financial goals.
10. **Recognizing that healing and liberation require economic justice**: Fundraising efforts should address economic disparities as part of broader social justice goals.

The national study by Dale and Hemachandra found that over 90% of survey respondents were familiar with CCF principles, and 76% reported that their organizations had changed fundraising practices in response to CCF or broader equity initiatives. Notably, 81% of organizations implementing CCF made changes across seven or more categories of CCF-aligned actions, indicating a holistic approach rather than isolated efforts. The most commonly adopted CCF practices included:

- Supporting other nonprofits' fundraising efforts (92%)
- Grounding fundraising in race, equity, and social justice (87%)
- Modifying storytelling practices to avoid harmful stereotypes (87%)
- Increasing accessibility in events and communications (86%)
- Changing internal operations to increase inclusion and equity (83%)

These principles encourage nonprofits to prioritize community empowerment over individual donor preferences, fostering a more equitable and sustainable approach to philanthropy. Most of us would agree with the overarching sentiment of these community-centric principles. It's their implementation and execution that gets complicated.

Case Study: Earthjustice's Journey Toward Equity

To see CCF in action, let's look at Earthjustice, a leading public interest law firm dedicated to environmental protection, which has embraced the principles of Community-Centric Fundraising to align its fundraising practices with its broader mission of racial and social equity. Under the leadership of Mollie Marsh-Heine, Senior Vice President of Development, the organization is methodically integrating these principles into its operations to address systemic inequities and foster authentic relationships with donors, staff, and community partners.

Challenges Addressed

- **Racial Inequities in Environmental Advocacy**: The environmental movement has historically been white-centered and white-led, often excluding communities of color from decision-making processes.
- **Wealth Disparities in Fundraising**: Traditional fundraising models often perpetuate economic inequities by focusing on high-net-worth donors without addressing systemic disparities.
- **Cultural Transformation**: Diversifying staff and leadership without creating an inclusive culture risks high turnover among employees from underrepresented backgrounds.

Key Strategies and Actions

Organizational Commitment to Anti-Racism

Earthjustice is undergoing a cultural transformation to become an anti-racist organization. This includes diversifying its staff and board, fostering an inclusive workplace culture, and aligning its practices with racial and social equity goals.

The development department plays a critical role by examining how fundraising can support anti-racist efforts while operating within an economic system that fosters wealth disparity.

Adopting Community-Centric Fundraising Principles

The team has committed to studying the 10 principles of CCF, dedicating monthly meetings to discuss each principle and evaluate alignment with their practices.

For example, Principle 6 ("Treat donors as partners") has been operationalized by engaging donors in transparent and sometimes challenging conversations about the intersectionality of environmental issues and racial justice.

Centering Clients and Communities

Earthjustice ensures that its legal work centers on the needs of its clients, often marginalized communities affected by environmental racism. For instance:

- In Louisiana's Cancer Alley, Earthjustice represents Black communities fighting petrochemical plants disproportionately sited in their neighborhoods.
- In wildlife litigation, tribal clients are highlighted as central stakeholders whose cultural and spiritual connections to habitats are integral to the cases.

Innovative Donor Engagement

Donors are encouraged to see beyond narrow interests (e.g., wildlife conservation) to understand the broader social justice context of Earthjustice's work.

Tactically, this involves crafting narratives that connect donors' passions (e.g., wolves or grizzlies) with systemic issues like historic injustices faced by Indigenous peoples.

Valuing Time as Much as Money

Earthjustice revamped its donor recognition practices to emphasize long-term commitment over monetary contributions. For example:

- The annual report now organizes donor lists by longevity rather than donation size.
- Volunteers' contributions are acknowledged alongside financial gifts, reflecting their equal importance.

Internal Capacity Building

Staff training on anti-racism, microaggressions, and restorative justice is mandatory for all employees.

New hires undergo foundational anti-racist training within six months to ensure alignment with organizational values.

Outcomes

- **Improved Donor Relationships:** Transparent conversations have deepened trust with donors while broadening their understanding of Earthjustice's mission.
- **Stronger Team Cohesion:** The fundraising team has become more connected through shared learning and open dialogue about difficult topics.
- **Positive Cultural Shifts:** By prioritizing inclusivity and equity, Earthjustice has created a more supportive environment for staff from diverse backgrounds.
- **Increased Community Impact:** Through partnerships with funding umbrellas and consortiums, Earthjustice channels resources to grassroots environmental justice organizations.

Contrary to concerns about financial risk, the impact of CCF-aligned changes was largely positive or neutral. Most organizations reported either increases or stability in contributed revenue, donor numbers, and volunteer engagement. While 26% of organizations lost some donors due to CCF-aligned changes, many were able to find new funding sources to replace them. Furthermore, nearly 45% of organizations reported increased fundraiser morale, with fewer than 5% noting a decrease. Although the research sample is relatively small, these findings offer promise.

Lessons Learned

- **Start Small but Be Consistent:** Earthjustice's gradual approach—focusing on one CCF principle at a time—has made the initiative manageable and sustainable.
- **Embrace Mistakes as Learning Opportunities:** A notable misstep involved printing case statements in font sizes too small for older donors—a $10,000 mistake that underscored the importance of audience testing.
- **Adapt Fundraising Practices for Equity:** Shifting from traditional donor-centric models to community-centric approaches requires ongoing reflection and adaptation.

Earthjustice's journey demonstrates that adopting community-centric fundraising is not only feasible but also transformative for organizations committed to equity and justice. By centering clients, fostering inclusive practices, and engaging donors as partners in systemic change, Earthjustice is setting a powerful example for nonprofits seeking to align their values with their operations.

As the CCF Movement Has Grown

As the community-centered fundraising (CCF) movement has grown, several key principles have emerged to guide its implementation effectively:

- **Prioritizing Community Well-Being:** Fundraising efforts should focus on addressing the needs of the community as a whole rather than prioritizing individual donor preferences.
- **Embracing Transparency:** Open communication with donors and stakeholders is essential to build trust and align expectations with equity-focused goals.
- **Recognizing the Value of All Forms of Contribution:** Contributions of time, expertise, and advocacy are equally important as financial donations in creating systemic change.
- **Fostering Inclusivity:** Fundraising practices must actively include diverse voices and perspectives, ensuring that marginalized communities are centered in decision-making processes.

The nonprofit community has been actively sharing experiences and strategies to implement these principles, leveraging new tools and technologies to advance equity-centered fundraising practices.

Challenges and Growing Pains

Of course, no revolution comes without its challenges. Despite the positive outcomes, the study by Elizabeth Dale and Maya Hemachandra identified five major barriers to CCF adoption:

- Resistance from boards and leadership unfamiliar with CCF principles
- Resource constraints and concerns about financial impact

- Limited staff capacity to implement changes
- Geographic and political considerations
- Structural challenges within the professional fundraising industry

Transitioning to a community-first approach has revealed several hurdles:

- **Resistance from Traditional Approaches:** Those accustomed to donor-centered models may hesitate to embrace change, fearing potential impacts on revenue or donor relationships.
- **Complexity in Measuring Success:** Evaluating the impact of CCF is akin to measuring the health of a forest rather than counting individual trees—qualitative outcomes often take precedence over quantitative metrics like dollars raised.
- **Donor Discomfort with Social Justice Messaging:** Emphasizing equity and justice may alienate some donors, though transparent communication has attracted new supporters who value these principles.

Despite these challenges, many organizations have found that adopting CCF fosters deeper connections with donors and communities while advancing systemic change. The movement continues to evolve as nonprofits share lessons learned and refine their approaches.

Let's examine the strengths and shadow side aspects of community-centered fundraising in Table 3.1.

The Dale and Hemachandra research also found that organizations with three or more BIPOC fundraisers were significantly more likely to adopt CCF practices, underscoring the importance of staff diversity in driving transformative change within nonprofit fundraising.

Main Criticisms of Community-Centered Fundraising

Community-centered fundraising (CCF), while lauded for its equity-driven approach, has sparked significant criticisms from practitioners and thought leaders in the nonprofit sector. Below is a summary of the key critiques:

Table 3.1 Strengths vs. Shadow Sides of Community-Centered Fundraising

Strengths	Shadow Side
Equity and Social Justice Focus: Addresses racial and economic injustices, promoting social change.	**Complex Implementation:** Requires significant changes in organizational culture and strategy.
Community Collaboration: Prioritizes collective community, enhancing interdependence and mutual support among nonprofits.	**Potential Funding Risks:** Focusing on community needs over donor preferences may reduce short-term funding.
Inclusive Fundraising Practices: Broadens potential support base by valuing non-financial contributions.	**Resistance from Traditional Donors:** Shifting to a community-centric model may lead to decreased funding.
Transparent and Honest Communication: Fosters meaningful relationships by treating donors as partners in addressing systemic issues.	**Measurement Difficulties:** Emphasizing qualitative outcomes can make demonstrating success to stakeholders challenging.
Encourages Sustainable Practices: Prioritizes long-term impact and adaptability, fostering enduring positive change.	**Systemic Barriers:** The broader philanthropic landscape dominated by traditional models and competitive culture poses adoption challenges.

Perpetuates a False Donor-Community Dichotomy

Critics argue that CCF creates an artificial divide between donors and communities, ignoring the reality that donors are often integral members of the broader community. Traditional donor-centric practices emphasize personalized stewardship to build trust and accountability, whereas CCF's framing risks alienating donors who could be allies in equity work. As one critic notes, "Donors are but one of many sources of power nonprofits navigate… most exert little pressure beyond expecting funds to be used as promised."

Lack of Clear Implementation Guidelines

CCF's principles have been criticized for being vague and abstract, offering limited actionable steps for fundraisers. Terms like "collective well-being" and "interdependence" are seen as nebulous, leaving organizations uncertain about how to operationalize equity without sacrificing revenue. This ambiguity risks performative adoption, where nonprofits rebrand existing practices as "community-centric" without addressing systemic power imbalances.

Ideological Over Practical Focus

Detractors contend that CCF prioritizes social justice rhetoric over fundraising efficacy. Critics of traditional models argue that:

- **Donor Motivations are Oversimplified:** CCF assumes donors primarily seek ego gratification, overlooking altruistic or community-minded intentions.
- **Systemic Critiques Lack Nuance:** By framing philanthropy as inherently colonialist, CCF dismisses incremental progress and shared goals between donors and nonprofits.

One critic asserts, "CCF confuses movement-building with fundraising mechanics, sidelining practical strategies that sustain nonprofits."

Risks to Revenue and Donor Relationships

CCF's rejection of "toxic dollars" (funding with harmful strings attached) is seen as financially untenable for resource-strapped nonprofits. Critics warn that:

- Donor alienation could reduce funding, especially if wealthier contributors perceive CCF's equity focus as accusatory.
- Marginalized-led organizations may disproportionately suffer due to their limited financial cushion to decline restrictive grants.

Undermining Fundraiser Expertise

Traditional practitioners argue that CCF dismisses decades of donor-centric research demonstrating how relationship-building increases retention and impact. Critics accuse CCF of "reinventing the wheel" without evidence that its model sustainably funds nonprofits. Rogare, a UK-based Fundraising Think Tank, highlights that CCF critiques philanthropy's entire system, making it "a clash of ideologies, not just fundraising tactics."

Balancing the Critique

Proponents acknowledge these challenges but argue that CCF is necessary to correct philanthropy's inequities. Vu Le counters that traditional fundraising's "default settings"—such as white savior narratives and wealth hoarding—perpetuate the very issues nonprofits aim to solve. While imperfect, CCF sparks critical conversations about power redistribution—a step many believe outweighs its implementation hurdles.

The debate reflects a tension between immediate practicality (fundraising within existing systems) and long-term systemic change (reimagining philanthropy's role in justice). As one critic concedes, "CCF's value lies in forcing fundraisers to confront uncomfortable truths, even if its solutions remain aspirational."

By embracing these critiques while continuing to refine practices, nonprofits can work toward integrating the strengths of both donor-centered and community-centered approaches into a more balanced framework.

Scaling Community-Centered Fundraising

While the findings of the *Adopting Community-Centric Fundraising: Findings from A National Study* underscore the viability of CCF as an alternative to traditional donor-centered fundraising for some organizations, they also reveal that community-centered fundraising has yet to be implemented at scale across the sector. Implementation practices remain vague and largely undocumented, and most participating organizations were human service nonprofits with budgets ranging from \$1M to \$5M located in large cities (over 300,000 people).

This research provides a foundation for ongoing exploration into how nonprofits can adopt CCF principles more broadly while addressing structural barriers and resource constraints.

By continuing to share lessons learned and refine implementation strategies, nonprofit leaders can work toward building a more equitable and inclusive philanthropic landscape that aligns with the values of community empowerment and justice.

Donor-Centered vs. Community-Centered Fundraising: A Comparison

Table 3.2 provides a clear and concise comparison of the two fundraising models, highlighting their distinct characteristics and the implications of adopting each approach within a nonprofit organization.

This framework helps us see how these approaches relate to each other and identifies potential integration points. The key is not to blindly adopt one model over another but to thoughtfully consider how we can blend their strengths while mitigating their weaknesses.

But how do we actually do this? How do we navigate the power dynamics, sustain engagement, and measure impact in a way that honors both donors and communities?

Blending the Best Parts: Toward a Human-Centered Approach

Reflecting on the nuanced landscape of donor-centered and community-centered fundraising, it's clear that this is a complex, multifaceted conversation. Each approach offers valuable insights and has its limitations, and finding balance requires thoughtful dialogue.

As fundraising professionals, we must critically examine our practices and motivations. Our goal should be to ensure that our efforts not only sustain our organizations but also genuinely contribute to the greater good. Through open conversations, diverse perspectives, and a commitment to continuous improvement, we can help shape a fundraising future that makes meaningful differences in our communities while advancing social justice.

Table 3.2 Donor-Centered vs. Community-Centered Fundraising

Aspect	Donor-Centered Fundraising (DCF)	Community-Centered Fundraising (CCF)
Core Focus	Building strong, personal relationships with donors.	Prioritizing community well-being and equity.
Key Principles	Personalization, donor appreciation, impact reporting.	Race, equity, social justice, mutual support, valuing all forms of contribution.
Emergence	Emerged in the late 1990s and early 2000s.	Developed more recently as a response to the limitations of DCF.
Goals	Enhance donor experience, ensure donors feel valued and involved.	Promote fairness, tackle systemic issues like racism and economic inequality.
Challenges	Potential ethical concerns, risk of perpetuating inequities, mission drift.	Implementation challenges, potential resistance from traditional donors, defining "community."
Advantages	Effective in boosting donations through strong donor relationships.	Focuses on broader social impact and inclusivity.
Limitations	May prioritize donor satisfaction at the expense of community needs, leading to transactional relationships.	Struggles with acceptance among traditional donors, potential impact on funding.

(continued)

Table 3.2   Donor-Centered vs. Community-Centered Fundraising *(continued)*

Aspect	Donor-Centered Fundraising (DCF)	Community-Centered Fundraising (CCF)
Measurement of Success	Often measured by the amount of funds raised and donor satisfaction.	Measured by the degree of community impact and advancement of equity and justice.
Technological Utilization	Uses technology to tailor interactions and enhance personalization.	Uses technology to foster community engagement and transparency.
Cultural and Social Alignment	Aligns fundraising efforts with donor values and expectations.	Aligns fundraising efforts with community needs and social justice principles.
Impact on Nonprofit Mission	Risk of mission drift if too focused on pleasing donors.	Aims to realign nonprofit efforts toward comprehensive community benefits.
Public Perception	Seen as traditional and donor-pleasing.	Viewed as progressive, focusing on systemic change and inclusivity.
Future Outlook	Continues to be popular but faces criticism for not adequately addressing community issues.	Gaining traction as more organizations seek to address broader community challenges.

Building Purpose-Driven Partnerships

As we explore ways to integrate donor-centered and community-centered approaches, fostering purpose-driven partnerships becomes essential. Fundraising expert Jim Langley reminds us that effective donor engagement isn't about pandering to donors' desires but about aligning shared values and demonstrating tangible impact.

Organizations should cultivate relationships with donors who view their contributions as investments in community progress rather than opportunities for personal recognition. This perspective complements community-centered fundraising by grounding donor relationships in mutual respect and shared purpose.

By prioritizing transparency and impact over recognition, nonprofits can build coalitions that advance equity while maintaining financial sustainability. These purpose-driven partnerships allow nonprofits to engage donors as collaborators in systemic change rather than mere financial supporters.

Moving Forward: The Promise of a New Paradigm

As we've explored the historical evolution and core principles of both donor-centered and community-centered fundraising, it's evident that each approach offers valuable insights but also presents significant limitations when implemented in isolation. The tension between these models reflects broader questions about power, equity, and effectiveness in the nonprofit sector.

What I propose is blending the best elements of both donor-centered and community-centered approaches, grounding our work in a profound respect for everyone involved. The essential question remains: *How can we effectively integrate these models? How can we harness the power of human connections and collective action to create a better world for all?*

These questions lead us to a transformative new framework that transcends this apparent dichotomy: *human-centered fundraising*. This approach synthesizes the strengths of both models while addressing their limitations, offering a more holistic and inclusive vision for mobilizing resources in service of social change.

By shifting our focus from philosophical camps to shared human connections, we can build fundraising practices that are not only more effective but also more aligned with our deepest values. The journey toward this integrated approach begins with the understanding that everyone involved in the philanthropic process—donors, community members, nonprofit staff, and volunteers—brings unique perspectives and contributions that deserve to be valued and respected.

Key Takeaways and Action Steps

As we reflect on the origins and evolution of community-centered fundraising (CCF), here are the key takeaways and immediate steps you can implement to integrate these principles into your work:

Key Takeaways

- **Community-Centered Fundraising Prioritizes Equity and Justice:** CCF challenges traditional donor-centered models by focusing on the collective well-being of communities and addressing systemic inequities.
- **Principles That Drive Change:** The 10 principles of CCF emphasize inclusivity, transparency, and collaboration, fostering a sense of belonging while promoting long-term transformation over short-term transactions.
- **Challenges Are Opportunities for Growth:** While implementation can be complex—requiring cultural shifts, resource allocation, and overcoming resistance—CCF provides a framework to reimagine philanthropy as a tool for justice.
- **Positive Outcomes Are Emerging:** Research shows that organizations adopting CCF practices often experience stable or increased revenue, improved morale among fundraisers, and stronger community impact.
- **A Balanced Approach Is Key:** While CCF offers transformative potential, blending its principles with elements of donor-centered fundraising can create a more sustainable and inclusive model.

Action Steps

- **Start Small with One Principle:** Choose one CCF principle—such as valuing time as much as money or modifying storytelling practices—and integrate it into your next campaign or event.
- **Engage Your Team in Equity Discussions:** Host regular meetings to discuss CCF principles, assess alignment with current practices, and identify areas for improvement.

- **Collaborate with Other Nonprofits:** Build partnerships to share resources, support each other's efforts, and strengthen the broader nonprofit ecosystem.
- **Be Transparent with Donors:** Communicate openly about your organization's commitment to equity and how it aligns with your mission. Invite donors to join you in advancing social justice goals.
- **Invest in Staff Training:** Equip your team with the tools they need to implement CCF effectively, including anti-racism training, inclusive communication strategies, and restorative practices.

By taking these steps, you can begin to align your fundraising practices with the values of equity and justice while building stronger connections with donors and communities alike.

The Need for a New Approach: Bridging Donor-Centered and Community-Centered Models

As we conclude our exploration of community-centered fundraising, it's clear that this approach has sparked critical conversations about equity, justice, and the power dynamics in philanthropy. By prioritizing community well-being and challenging traditional donor-centric practices, community-centered fundraising has laid the groundwork for a more inclusive and equitable nonprofit sector. However, as we've seen, implementing these principles is not without its challenges—resistance from stakeholders, resource constraints, and the need for clearer strategies remain significant hurdles.

This brings us to an important question: *What's next?* How can we address the limitations of both donor-centered and community-centered models while building on their strengths? Is there a way to create a fundraising approach that values donors, empowers communities, and fosters meaningful connections?

This tension highlights a critical need for a new approach—one that synthesizes the strengths of both models while addressing their limitations. Enter **human-centered fundraising**, a framework that places shared humanity at its core. By prioritizing mutual respect, inclusivity, and collaboration, human-centered fundraising seeks to honor the contributions of every stakeholder—donors, community members, nonprofit staff, and volunteers—while advancing systemic change. Human-centered fundraising offers a way forward by:

- **Blending Personalization with Equity:** It respects donors' motivations while ensuring that fundraising practices align with social justice goals.
- **Fostering Shared Purpose:** It builds coalitions of donors and communities united by a common vision for impact.
- **Prioritizing Long-Term Transformation:** It moves beyond transactional relationships to focus on sustainable change driven by collective action.

Overall, the Dale and Maya study findings indicate that CCF represents a viable alternative to traditional donor-centered fundraising—one capable of maintaining financial sustainability while building more equitable and inclusive philanthropic practices. However, the movement's continued evolution will depend on addressing persistent barriers and scaling implementation beyond early adopters.

In Chapter 4, we'll explore how the emerging human-centered fundraising paradigm seeks to blend the best elements of both approaches. By focusing on shared humanity and mutual respect, human-centered fundraising offers a path forward—one that unlocks greater impact, mobilizes resources more effectively, and makes fundraising practices more inclusive and engaging.

We'll examine how this approach can redefine relationships between donors, nonprofits, and communities while addressing systemic challenges in philanthropy. Together, let's envision a future where fundraising is not just a transaction but a powerful tool for connection and collective action.

4 | The Need for a New Approach: Human-Centered Fundraising

"In any given moment we have two options: to step forward into growth or step back into safety."
—Abraham Maslow, American Psychologist and Philosopher

The world of fundraising is at a crossroads. Thought leaders like Vu Le advocate for a shift away from traditional donor-centered fundraising, while Penelope Burk, Ken Burnett, and others stand firm in their belief in the donor-centered, relationship-focused fundraising approach. Instead of choosing a path, we may need to build a wider road. A road wide enough to accommodate us all in a human-centered approach, dedicated to meeting the collective needs of donors, beneficiaries, staff, and communities alike. An approach that fosters understanding, belonging, equity, inclusion, and shared impact-building on the best of community-centered and donor-centered approaches.

At first glance, community-centered fundraising and donor-centered fundraising seem like opposing philosophies. Community-centered fundraising focuses on equity, collective impact, and addressing systemic issues, while donor-centered fundraising prioritizes building deep relationships with individual donors. Unfortunately, donor-centered fundraising can sometimes lead to mission drift, reinforce biases and stereotypes, and perpetuate systemic inequities. It can also create a transactional dynamic that overlooks the voices of those served.

This chapter explores how human-centered fundraising offers a powerful way to bridge these divides. It calls on all of us—fundraisers, nonprofit leaders, donors, and community members to come together, speak truth to power, and collectively create a more just and effective philanthropic ecosystem.

The Core Principles of Human-Centered Fundraising

Before we dive deeper, let's establish the foundational pillars of human-centered fundraising. These principles will serve as your guide throughout this chapter and beyond:

- **Empathy:** Center the needs, perspectives, and lived experiences of all stakeholders: donors, beneficiaries, staff, and community members-in every decision and interaction.
- **Equity and Inclusion:** Actively address systemic inequities, ensuring that fundraising practices are accessible and inclusive for people from all backgrounds.
- **Collaboration and Co-Creation:** Involve stakeholders in designing, implementing, and evaluating fundraising strategies to foster shared ownership and innovation.
- **Transparency:** Communicate openly about goals, impact, and decision-making processes to build trust and accountability.
- **Holistic Impact:** Value all forms of contribution-time, talent, networks, advocacy, and financial support, and recognize the interconnectedness of the philanthropic ecosystem.
- **Continuous Learning and Iteration:** Embrace feedback, adapt to changing needs, and refine strategies for greater effectiveness.

Unlocking Greater Impact Through Human-Centered Fundraising

Imagine combining the powers of two superhero teams—the Donor Defenders and the Community Champions—into a new breed of fundraising superheroes who harness the best of both worlds. Human-centered fundraising is that new approach. It integrates the strengths of donor-centered and community-centered fundraising to create a holistic, inclusive, and impactful model.

Let's face it—the world of fundraising can sometimes feel like a tug-of-war between different philosophies. On one side, we have donor-centered fundraising, which focuses on building deep relationships with individual donors and making them feel valued. On the other side, there's community-centered fundraising, which emphasizes equity, collective impact, and addressing systemic issues.

Both approaches have their merits, but they also have their limitations. Donor-centered fundraising can sometimes prioritize wealthy individuals at the expense of broader community engagement. Community-centered fundraising, while noble in its intentions, can struggle to secure the large donations often required for significant projects.

That's where human-centered fundraising comes in. It's like being a master chef, taking the finest ingredients from both approaches and creating a gourmet meal that's greater than the sum of its parts.

The Power of Integration

Human-centered fundraising recognizes that donors, beneficiaries, staff, and community members are all integral parts of the philanthropic ecosystem. By valuing everyone's contributions and perspectives, we create a more holistic and impactful approach to fundraising.

For example, let's look at how the American Heart Association (AHA) has embraced elements of human-centered fundraising. Traditionally known for its donor-centered approach, the AHA has, in recent years, expanded its focus to include community-driven initiatives. Their "Go Red for Women" campaign not only raises funds but also empowers women to take charge of their heart health, creating a movement that goes beyond just writing checks.

Building Bridges, Not Walls

One of the key benefits of human-centered fundraising is its ability to bridge divides. Instead of pitting community members against donors or beneficiaries against staff, it creates a collaborative environment where everyone's strengths are valued.

I once worked with a small environmental nonprofit struggling to balance the desires of major donors with community needs. By adopting a human-centered approach, they brought both groups together, organizing field trips where donors could see the impact of their contributions firsthand and meet community members taking action for environmental conservation. This increased donor engagement and ensured programs truly met community needs.

Embracing Diversity and Inclusion

Human-centered fundraising inherently promotes diversity and inclusion. By valuing all forms of contribution—not just monetary donations—it opens the door for broader participation. This can lead to a more diverse donor base and more representative voices in decision-making processes.

For instance, a youth-focused nonprofit I advised implemented a youth advisory board, giving beneficiaries a say in program development and fundraising strategies. This improved programs and attracted new donors who were impressed by the organization's commitment to youth empowerment and inspired by the youth themselves.

Community-Centered Fundraising: Building Common Ground

Community-centered fundraising, as championed by Vu Le, emphasizes building authentic relationships with communities and addressing systemic inequities. It challenges nonprofits to move beyond transactional donor relationships and focus on equity, inclusion, and collective impact.

This approach calls on organizations to listen deeply to community needs, share power, and co-create solutions. It encourages fundraisers to be advocates for justice and equity, ensuring that fundraising practices do not perpetuate harm or exclusion.

By integrating community-centered principles with donor-centered strengths, human-centered fundraising creates a balanced, ethical, and effective model for resource mobilization.

How Human-Centered Fundraising Can Mobilize Resources

Now that we understand the philosophy behind human-centered fundraising, let's talk about how it can supercharge your resource mobilization efforts. Think of it as upgrading from a bicycle to a rocket ship-you're still heading in the same direction, but you'll get there faster and with a lot more excitement!

Expanding the Definition of "Resources"

One of the most powerful aspects of human-centered fundraising is that it expands our understanding of what constitutes a valuable resource. Money is important, of course, but it's not the only thing that matters. I firmly believe that time is far more valuable than money—I can make more money. I haven't yet figured out how to make more time.

Time, skills, networks, and advocacy are all crucial resources that can drive your mission forward. By recognizing and valuing these contributions, you can tap into a much broader pool of support.

For instance, I worked with a homeless shelter that started a "Skills Bank" program. Community members could donate their professional skills—from legal advice to haircuts—to help shelter residents. This not only provided valuable services but also created a sense of community involvement that led to increased financial donations.

Creating a Culture of Philanthropy

Human-centered fundraising isn't just about changing tactics—it's about shifting the entire culture of your organization. When everyone—from the board to community volunteers—sees themselves as part of the fundraising process, magic happens.

I once consulted with a small arts organization that was struggling to meet its fundraising goals. By adopting a human-centered approach, they transformed their entire staff into fundraising ambassadors. The marketing team started sharing powerful impact stories on social media. The program staff began welcoming donors to see their work in action. From the Executive Director to the maintenance staff, everyone began to see the importance of their unique role in the overall engagement of their community.

The result? A 30% increase in donations in just one year and a more engaged and motivated staff.

Leveraging Technology and Responsible AI

In our digital age, technology can be a powerful tool for human-centered fundraising. Crowdfunding platforms, for example, have revolutionized grassroots fundraising by allowing organizations to tell their stories directly to potential donors, create urgency, and show real-time progress toward goals.

But technology should enhance human connection, not replace it. Use digital tools to start conversations, then follow up with personal interactions.

Responsible AI Use

Artificial intelligence (AI) is increasingly used in fundraising for donor segmentation, personalized outreach, and process automation. However, it's vital to use AI responsibly—ensuring transparency, avoiding bias, and protecting constituent data. Organizations should establish clear policies for the responsible use of AI, regularly audit algorithms for fairness, and prioritize the human element in relationship-building at all times.

But remember, technology should enhance human connection, not replace it. Use digital tools to start conversations, then follow up with personal interactions.

Case Studies of Human-Centered Fundraising Success

To illustrate the power of human-centered fundraising in action, let's look at two organizations that have successfully implemented this approach:

Cycle for Survival—Memorial Sloan Kettering Cancer Center

Cycle for Survival exemplifies how human-centered fundraising can create a powerful movement by combining personal storytelling with community engagement:

- Founded by a cancer patient and her spouse, creating a deeply personal connection
- Grew from 230 participants, raising $250,000, to over 30,000 riders, raising $34 million in 2017

- Focuses on rare cancer research, giving participants a clear, impactful mission
- Utilizes indoor cycling events across multiple cities, making participation accessible
- Raised over $320 million since 2007, demonstrating long-term sustainability

What makes Cycle for Survival a prime example of human-centered fundraising is its ability to blend the personal touch of donor-centered approaches with the community-building aspect of community-centered fundraising. By creating an event that allows participants to honor loved ones affected by cancer while also being part of a larger community effort, Cycle for Survival taps into both individual motivations and collective impact.

James Beard Foundation

The James Beard Foundation's partnership with CCS Fundraising showcases how a shift toward a more human-centered model can transform an organization's fundraising efforts:

- Transitioned from event-based revenue to a philanthropy-driven model
- Created a new case for support aligned with their renewed mission
- Expanded their development team from two to six people
- Secured two seven-figure pledges, the largest individual donations in their history
- Launched their most ambitious fundraising campaign, raising 30% of the goal early in the campaign

The James Beard Foundation's success demonstrates how human-centered fundraising can lead to more sustainable and impactful giving. By aligning their fundraising efforts with their mission and engaging donors in a more meaningful way, they were able to secure larger donations and build a stronger foundation for future growth.

These case studies illustrate how human-centered fundraising can lead to remarkable results when implemented thoughtfully. By focusing on personal connections, clear impact, and accessible participation methods, organizations can create fundraising initiatives that resonate deeply with both individual donors and the broader community.

Making Fundraising Practices More Efficient, Inclusive, and Engaging

Now, I know what you might be thinking. "This all sounds great in theory, but how does it work in practice?" Well, buckle up because we're about to get into the nitty-gritty of how human-centered fundraising can transform your day-to-day operations.

Streamlining Your Processes

One of the beautiful things about human-centered fundraising is that it can actually make your life easier. By focusing on building genuine relationships and creating meaningful experiences, you can often reduce the need for constant, uncomfortable, high-pressure asks.

For example, I worked with a wildlife conservation organization that was spending a fortune on direct mail campaigns with diminishing returns. We shifted their strategy to focus on creating immersive experiences for donors: in-person and virtual reality tours of wildlife habitats, live webcams of animal rescues, and behind-the-scenes looks at their work.

The result? They were able to reduce their direct mail budget by 50% while increasing overall donations. Donors were more engaged, more likely to give repeatedly, and more inclined to share their experiences with friends.

Fostering Inclusivity

Human-centered fundraising is inherently more inclusive than traditional models. By valuing all forms of contribution and actively seeking diverse perspectives, you create a more welcoming environment for supporters from all walks of life.

Consider the case of a community health clinic I advised. They implemented a "Community Health Ambassador" program, allowing patients to volunteer and share their stories to support educational outreach and awareness efforts across their community. This not only improved their connection with the community but also led to more culturally sensitive fundraising appeals and programs.

Boosting Engagement Through Storytelling

At its heart, human-centered fundraising is about telling compelling stories that connect people to your cause. By focusing on the human impact of your work, you can create emotional connections that inspire action.

I once worked with a literacy nonprofit that was struggling to articulate its impact. We shifted their focus from dry statistics to powerful personal stories. They started featuring video testimonials from adult learners who had overcome literacy challenges, sharing how it had transformed their lives and their families. From securing better-paying jobs to the joy of reading to their children and grandchildren, their confidence and overall quality of life multiplied.

The impact was immediate and profound. Donation rates increased, but more importantly, so did volunteer applications and community partnerships. People weren't just giving money—they were making meaningful connections and becoming part of the story.

Challenges and Solutions in Implementing Human-Centered Fundraising

Now, I won't sugarcoat it—implementing a human-centered approach isn't always a walk in the park. Like any significant change, it comes with its own set of challenges. But don't worry, I've got your back. Let's look at some common hurdles and how to overcome them.

Challenge 1: Resistance to Change

You might encounter staff or board members who are comfortable with the status quo and resistant to new approaches.

Solution: Start small and show results. Begin with a pilot project that demonstrates the effectiveness of human-centered fundraising. Use data and stories to make your case. Remember, seeing (and feeling) is believing!

Challenge 2: Balancing Donor Desires with Community Needs

Sometimes, what major donors want doesn't align perfectly with what the community needs.

Solution: Create opportunities for dialogue and deeper understanding. Organize events where donors can collaborate with community members. Help donors see the bigger picture and understand how their support, along with the support of others, contributes to systemic change.

Challenge 3: Resource Constraints

Implementing new strategies often requires time and resources that might seem scarce.

Solution: Remember, human-centered fundraising is about working smarter, not necessarily harder. Look for ways to integrate this approach into existing activities. Can your annual gala include elements of community storytelling? Can your next newsletter feature voices from program participants? How can artificial intelligence help streamline processes and automate routine tasks to allow staff to reallocate their time to community relationship building?

Challenge 4: Measuring Impact

Traditional fundraising metrics might not capture the full value of a human-centered approach.

Solution: Develop new metrics that reflect your holistic goals. This might include measures of community engagement, volunteer retention rates, or increasing the diversity of your supporter base. Remember, what gets measured gets managed!

Potential Limitations and How to Address Them

While human-centered fundraising offers many benefits, it is not without challenges:

- **Risk of Mission Drift:** Balancing diverse stakeholder needs can sometimes pull organizations away from their core mission.
  - Mitigation: Regularly revisit and reaffirm your mission in all fundraising activities.
- **Resource Intensiveness:** Co-creation and inclusive practices can require more time and staff capacity.
  - Mitigation: Prioritize actions, start small, and build capacity over time.

- **Difficulty Balancing Stakeholder Needs:** It can be challenging to give equal voice to donors, beneficiaries, and staff.
    - Mitigation: Establish clear decision-making processes and transparent communication channels.

Integrating Human-Centered Fundraising with Organizational Strategy

Human-centered fundraising isn't just a set of tactics-it's a lens for your entire organization. To fully realize its potential:

- Embed human-centered principles into your mission, vision, and values statements.
- Ensure governance structures (e.g., board composition, decision-making processes) reflect a genuine commitment to equity and inclusion.
- Align fundraising goals and evaluation methods with broader organizational strategy.
- Foster a culture where staff at all levels are empowered to contribute ideas and feedback.

Rethinking Metrics: Measuring What Matters

Traditional fundraising metrics-like dollars raised or number of donors-don't tell the whole story. Consider adding new qualitative and quantitative indicators, such as:

- **Community Engagement:** Number of community members involved in fundraising planning or events.
- **Diversity of Supporters:** Demographic data on donors, volunteers, and beneficiaries.
- **Volunteer Retention Rates:** How many volunteers return year after year.
- **Stakeholder Satisfaction:** Surveys or interviews with donors, beneficiaries, and staff.
- **Storytelling Impact:** Engagement rates on stories shared (e.g., views, shares, qualitative feedback).

Collect this data through surveys, focus groups, CRM systems, and regular check-ins. Use the insights to refine your approach and demonstrate holistic impact.

Navigating Ethical Considerations in Human-Centered Fundraising

As we embrace the human-centered approach to fundraising, it's crucial to address the ethical implications that arise when balancing donor desires with community needs. This approach requires careful consideration of various stakeholders' interests and a commitment to ethical, inclusive decision-making.

Balancing Donor and Community Interests

Human-centered fundraising seeks to find common ground between donor expectations and community impact. This involves:

- Engaging in transparent communication with donors and community members
- Aligning organizational goals with the values of all stakeholders
- Demonstrating impact in ways that satisfy donors while prioritizing community needs

Ethical Challenges and Solutions

Nonprofit organizations often face ethical dilemmas in fundraising. Some common challenges include:

- Compensation issues, especially for leadership roles
- Conflicts of interest, particularly involving board members
- Transparency in fund allocation
- Accepting donations from controversial or questionable sources
- The ethical use of constituent data
- Responsible and transparent use of artificial intelligence

To address these challenges, organizations should:

- Develop clear policies on compensation and reimbursement
- Implement strict conflict of interest policies and disclosure requirements

- Maintain transparency in financial reporting and fund usage
- Establish a gift acceptance policy, including a morality clause
- Develop a constituent personal data privacy policy

Moving Beyond Donor-Centrism

While donor-centered practices have their merits, it's important to recognize the potential ethical pitfalls of prioritizing donors above all else. Human-centered fundraising encourages a more balanced approach that:

- Considers the needs and perspectives of all stakeholders, including beneficiaries
- Avoids perpetuating systemic inequities through fundraising practices
- Empowers communities to have a voice in how funds are raised and used

By addressing these ethical considerations, human-centered fundraising can create a more equitable and sustainable approach to nonprofit resource mobilization.

Key Takeaways and Action Steps

Key Takeaways

1. Human-Centered Fundraising Bridges Philosophies Combines the best of donor-centered and community-centered fundraising to build a more equitable, inclusive, and impactful approach.
2. Core Principles Define the Practice:
   - Empathy
   - Equity and Inclusion
   - Collaboration and Co-Creation
   - Transparency
   - Holistic Impact
   - Continuous Learning
3. It Expands the Definition of "Resources" Values time, skills, networks, and advocacy—not just money—thus unlocking new avenues of engagement.
4. Creates a Culture of Philanthropy Engages all staff, volunteers, and community members in fundraising, leading to increased morale and donor support.

5. **Technology Must Enhance, Not Replace, Connection** Use tech and AI responsibly—to automate, personalize, and streamline—while keeping relationship-building at the center.

6. **Success Stories Demonstrate the Power**
   - Cycle for Survival shows grassroots momentum and emotional storytelling.
   - James Beard Foundation showcases mission alignment, major gifts growth, and campaign success.

7. **Improves Inclusion and Engagement**
   Human-centered practices naturally invite broader participation and ensure fundraising efforts reflect community voices.

8. **Challenges Are Real—But Solvable**
   Resistance, resource constraints, and measuring impact are addressed through pilots, strategic alignment, and redefining metrics.

9. **Ethics Are Non-Negotiable**
   A human-centered lens requires proactive attention to ethical issues, such as compensation, data use, and balancing donor and community interests.

10. **It's a Cultural Shift, Not Just a Tactic**
    True adoption means embedding principles in governance, team composition, strategy, and storytelling.

Action Steps

1. Audit Current Practices
   - Assess where your organization currently sits on the donor-centered vs. community-centered spectrum.
   - Identify opportunities to incorporate more human-centered principles.

2. Develop or Revisit Core Documents
   - Integrate human-centered values into your mission, vision, and fundraising strategy.
   - Establish or update ethics policies: gift acceptance, data privacy, conflict of interest.

3. Pilot a Human-Centered Fundraising Initiative
   - Start small (e.g., community storytelling in your appeal, co-created donor event).
   - Gather feedback and measure results beyond dollars (e.g., engagement, diversity of participation).
4. Invest in Staff Development
   - Train team members on empathy-driven communication, responsible AI use, and ethical fundraising practices.
   - Foster cross-functional collaboration between program and fundraising teams.
5. Rethink Metrics
   - Add new KPIs: stakeholder satisfaction, story engagement, diversity of supporters, volunteer retention.
   - Use surveys, CRM systems, and interviews to collect data.
6. Leverage Technology with Care
   - Use AI tools for segmentation, personalization, and automation—but maintain transparency and human follow-up.
   - Establish guardrails for responsible AI use (e.g., bias audits, data protection).
7. Engage Donors and Communities Together
   - Create opportunities for shared experiences, such as service days or storytelling events that involve both donors and beneficiaries.
8. Tell Better Stories
   - Shift from stats to stories—especially those that reflect diverse voices and lived experiences.
   - Include program participants, volunteers, and staff as narrators.
9. Build a Diverse Fundraising Team
   - Recruit and engage staff and board members who reflect the communities you serve.
   - Empower youth, clients, and community members with real influence in fundraising strategy.
10. Commit to the Journey
    - Treat human-centered fundraising as a long-term cultural shift.
    - Celebrate small wins, iterate often, and keep learning.

Embracing Human-Centered Fundraising: The Journey Ahead

As we wrap up this chapter, I hope you're feeling inspired and empowered to embrace human-centered fundraising. Remember, this isn't about throwing out everything you know. It's about evolving your approach to create something more impactful, more inclusive, and ultimately more successful.

Think of it as upgrading your fundraising superpowers. You're not just asking for money anymore—you're building a community-wide movement, creating connections, and changing lives. And isn't that why we got into this work in the first place?

In the next chapter, we'll dive into the practical steps of building a diverse fundraising team that can bring this human-centered approach to life. We'll explore how to assemble your own "League of Fundraising Heroes," each with their unique strengths and perspectives.

So, are you ready to take your fundraising to the next level? To create deeper connections, mobilize more resources, and make a bigger impact? Then turn the page because your human-centered fundraising journey is just beginning.

Human-Centered Fundraising in Practice

These chapters discuss the practical implementation of the human-centered model, including team building, storytelling, donor engagement, and the integration of technology.

5 | Assembling the Heroes: Building a Diverse Fundraising Team

"The work of inclusive philanthropy isn't a moment. It's a movement. And movements are sustained by people who are willing to lead with courage, to challenge the norms and to hold the line, stand ten toes down in equity, even when the tide shifts."
—Maia McGill, Founder and CEO, Inclusive Philanthropy Institute, Advocate for Historically Excluded Communities, Faculty, Modern Institute for Charitable Giving

I've met countless nonprofit leaders and fundraisers over the years. Each one of them, a hero in their own right, has worked tirelessly to make the world a better place. But even heroes need a strong team beside them, and that's what this chapter is all about—assembling your own league of fundraising superheroes.

The Power of Diversity in Fundraising Staff

Imagine your organization as a team of superheroes, each member bringing their own unique strengths—or superpowers—to the table. These superpowers might include cultural intelligence, innovative thinking, deep community connections, or specialized technical skills. Just as every superhero team thrives on the distinct abilities of its members, your diverse fundraising team has the potential to achieve extraordinary results by collectively leveraging these unique talents.

A truly effective fundraising team reflects a broad spectrum of backgrounds, perspectives, and lived experiences. Diversity is not just a buzzword—it is a strategic asset that drives creativity, innovation, and resilience. When team members bring different skills, cultures, and networks, they unlock new opportunities and approaches to fundraising challenges.

In this chapter, we'll explore how to assemble your own League of Heroes—a dynamic and diverse fundraising team that works together to tackle challenges, connect with donors and community members to amplify your mission's impact.

Reflection Questions

Take a moment to consider your current fundraising team:

- How well does it reflect the diversity of the communities you serve?
- What perspectives might be missing?
- Do they embody the core values of your organization?
- What skills do they possess, and what skills are collectively missing in our rapidly evolving profession?
- What expertise, experience, or influence do you need to take your fundraising strategy to the next level in the next 3, 5, or even 10 years?

Why Diversity Matters in Fundraising

Building a diverse fundraising team is about more than representation; it's about assembling a group of heroes whose combined superpowers create a force for innovation and transformation. Jim Collins, in *Good to Great and the Social Sectors*, emphasizes the critical importance of "getting the right people on the bus" and having them in the "right seats" for organizations in the social sector. He adapted this principle from his business-focused work to address the unique challenges faced by nonprofits, government agencies, and other mission-driven organizations.

Collins argued that the key to success in the social sector begins with identifying and placing the right leaders in positions where they can make the greatest impact. He stressed that having "the right people in the right seats" is not just about filling roles but ensuring alignment with organizational values and mission. This discipline is critical because it allows organizations to adapt and thrive despite constraints or external challenges. For Collins, this approach is foundational to transforming good organizations into great ones, even within the resource-limited and complex environment of the social sector. I don't think many of us would argue his brilliant insight. In addition, I contend that diversity is an often-overlooked characteristic of great teams or an afterthought at best.

Here are some reasons why I believe diversity is a superpower for fundraising teams:

- **Fresh Perspectives and Innovation:** When you bring together people with different experiences and viewpoints, creativity flourishes. Diverse teams generate innovative solutions to fundraising challenges that might never emerge from a more homogeneous group.
- **Authentic Donor Connections:** A team that reflects your community's diversity can forge genuine connections with a wider range of donors, leading to more meaningful relationships and increased support. Dr. Robert Cialdini is best known for his book *Influence: The Psychology of Persuasion*. Originally published in 1984, it has become a seminal work in the fields of psychology, marketing, and persuasion. The book explores the psychological principles behind why people say "yes" and how these principles can be applied ethically in various settings. It introduces six key principles of influence—Reciprocation, Commitment and Consistency, Social Proof, Liking, Authority, and Scarcity—with a seventh principle, Unity, added in the latest expanded edition.
- **Better Decision-Making:** Research confirms that diverse teams make better decisions. Multiple viewpoints lead to more thorough analysis and well-rounded strategies.

- **Cultural Intelligence:** A diverse team brings valuable cultural knowledge, helping your organization navigate sensitive issues and communicate respectfully and effectively with various communities.
- **Living Your Values:** For many nonprofits, equity and inclusion are central to their mission. A diverse team demonstrates authentic commitment to these values, both internally and externally.
- **Futureproofing:** As communities become increasingly diverse, successful nonprofits need a diverse donor base to sustain and grow their operations. A diverse team positions you to connect with current and emerging donor demographics.

Cialdini's principle of **Social Proof** refers to the psychological and social phenomenon where individuals look to the behavior and actions of others to determine the correct way to act, especially in situations of uncertainty or ambiguity. Social Proof is particularly powerful when:

- **Uncertainty** is high, as people are unsure of the correct decision or behavior.
- **Similarity** exists between the individual and the group, as people are more likely to follow those they perceive as similar to themselves.

Applying this psychology, it's more likely that we will attract diverse donors when they see diverse board representation, executive leadership, directors, managers, and front-line staff—*including fundraisers.*

By recognizing and celebrating these superpowers, you're not just building a team—you're assembling a League of Heroes ready to take on any challenge.

Reflection Questions

- Which of these diversity benefits resonates most with your organization's current needs?
- How might increased diversity address specific challenges you're facing?

Building Your Dream Team: Recruitment Strategies

When recruiting for your League of Heroes, think beyond traditional credentials and focus on identifying individuals with unique superpowers that complement your mission. Whether it's someone with deep ties to local communities, expertise in digital fundraising, or a knack for storytelling, each hero brings something special to the table.

Casting a Wider Net

Seek out heroes from historically excluded and underrepresented communities who can bring fresh perspectives and expand your organization's reach. Look beyond traditional job boards to find diverse talent:

- Utilize specialized platforms like the African American Development Officers Network (AADO), founded by Birgit Burton, Immediate Past Chair of the AFP Global Board
- Build relationships with professional associations serving underrepresented groups
- Partner with alumni networks and community organizations
- Leverage LinkedIn to identify and recruit individuals with the skills and attributes to strengthen your team

Craft Inclusive Job Descriptions

Highlight how your organization values each hero's unique contributions and is committed to creating an inclusive headquarters where all heroes can thrive. Your job postings create critical first impressions:

- Use inclusive language that welcomes all qualified candidates
- Focus on essential qualifications rather than extensive wish lists
- Explicitly state your organization's commitment to building an inclusive workplace
- Highlight flexible work arrangements when possible
- Post salary ranges to demonstrate your commitment to pay equity

From the Field: When Community Health Partners revamped their job descriptions to remove internal jargon and exclusionary language where possible, applications from people of color increased by 67%. Their development director noted, "We realized we were inadvertently signaling who we thought belonged here through our language choices."

Implement Bias-Free Hiring Practices

Unconscious bias can undermine even well-intentioned recruitment efforts:

- Conduct blind resume reviews by removing identifying information
- Use structured interviews with consistent questions for all candidates
- Ensure diverse interview panels to provide multiple perspectives
- Evaluate candidates against clear, job-relevant criteria

Look Beyond Traditional Credentials

Remember that diversity encompasses experiences and skills, not just demographics:

- Consider career-changers who bring fresh insights and transferable skills
- Value community activists and volunteers with deep local connections
- Recognize that lived experiences may be equally or more valuable than credentials in some cases
- Assess candidates for cultural add (not just cultural fit)

Recruitment on a Budget

Many nonprofits face resource constraints, but diversity initiatives don't have to break the bank:

- Partner with local colleges and universities for internship programs
- Leverage board and volunteer networks for candidate referrals
- Network at community events where fundraising professionals will be in attendance
- Focus on retaining top talent to reduce costly turnover (more on this below)

Building a diverse team is only the first step. To unlock the full potential of your team's diversity, fostering collaboration and unity is essential. In Chapter 6, "The League of Heroes Paradigm: Unity in Diversity," we'll explore practical strategies for breaking down silos and creating a culture of teamwork that amplifies individual strengths.

Reflection Questions

- Which of these recruitment strategies could you implement immediately, even with limited resources?
- What barriers might you face, and how could you overcome them?

Creating an Inclusive Culture

Recruitment is only the beginning. Your League of Heroes needs more than just recruitment—it needs a headquarters where every hero feels supported, valued, and empowered to use their superpowers. Creating an inclusive culture ensures that your heroes can collaborate effectively and continue growing their abilities.

Foster Belonging and Inclusion

- Celebrate each hero's unique contributions while building trust and camaraderie among team members
- Create spaces for team members to share perspectives and ideas freely
- Recognize and honor different cultural celebrations and traditions
- Provide ongoing training on recognizing and addressing subtle forms of discrimination
- Ensure all voices are heard and valued in meetings and decision-making

Provide Growth and Development

- Offer training programs that help heroes hone their superpowers and prepare them for leadership roles within your organization
- Pair newer team members with experienced fundraisers through mentoring programs
- Create clear advancement paths and actively support diverse team members in pursuing leadership roles
- Provide regular, constructive feedback focused on individual and team growth

Embrace Flexibility

Different team members have varying needs and responsibilities:

- Recognize that even superheroes need balance—offer flexible work arrangements so your heroes can recharge and perform at their best

- Consider adjustable schedules to accommodate personal commitments
- Implement supportive policies for team members with caregiving responsibilities
- Focus on results rather than rigid work structures

Continuously Improve

Creating an inclusive culture requires ongoing attention:

- Conduct regular surveys to gauge team satisfaction
- Use exit interviews to understand and address inclusivity challenges
- Track and report diversity metrics to measure progress
- Celebrate successes while acknowledging areas for growth

Reflection Questions

- How inclusive is your current organizational culture?
- What one change could you make this week to foster a greater sense of belonging for all team members?

Case Study: The Transformative Power of Diversity

Let's look at how one environmental nonprofit put their diverse team into action. Faced with raising $1 million for a conservation project when their traditional donor base was exhausted, their varied approaches yielded impressive results:

- Gabriela, a first-generation immigrant, forged partnerships with local ethnic business associations, opening new donor networks
- James, a former tech executive, developed a crowdfunding campaign leveraging social media influencers
- Aisha, with her background in community organizing, created neighborhood events that engaged grassroots supporters
- Christine, a long-time fundraiser of color with a strong history of major donor development, began engaging black leaders to join agency committees and eventually the board of directors

By combining these diverse strategies, the team exceeded their $1 million goal by 20% while building lasting relationships with previously untapped communities. This success demonstrates how diverse perspectives and networks achieve extraordinary results.

Reflection Question

How could a more diverse team help your organization reach new donors and volunteers, tackle fundraising challenges, and engage your community in innovative ways?

Measuring Diversity Impact: The Numbers That Matter

Beyond anecdotes, how do you know your diversity efforts are working? Here's a framework for measuring success:

Team Composition Metrics

- Demographic diversity across various dimensions (race, gender, age, neurodiversity, geography, etc.)
- Diversity at different levels of the organization (Board and Committees, Executive Leadership, Directors, Managers, etc.)
- Retention rates for team members from underrepresented groups (overall churn rate comparison to diverse team member churn rate)

Fundraising Performance Indicators

- New donor acquisition from diverse communities
- Retention rates across different donor demographics
- Growth in average gift size from underrepresented donor groups

Organizational Culture Measures

- Team member satisfaction scores
- Inclusivity ratings in anonymous surveys
- Participation in diversity initiatives

Reflection Questions

- Which of these metrics would be most meaningful for your organization?
- Are there other metrics you would add to measure progress in diversity?
- How could you start tracking them, even with limited resources?

Overcoming Common Challenges

Building and maintaining a diverse fundraising team comes with challenges. Here's how to address them:

Addressing Resistance to Change

Some team or board members may hesitate to embrace new approaches:

- Educate stakeholders on the benefits of diversity in fundraising
- Share success stories and data demonstrating diverse teams' impact
- Implement changes gradually, allowing time for adjustment
- Connect diversity initiatives directly to mission fulfillment and fundraising goals

Common Objection: "We just need the best fundraisers, regardless of background."

Evidence-Based Response: Research consistently shows diverse teams outperform homogeneous ones, even when individual team members have similar qualifications. Diversity itself is a performance multiplier that leads to better problem-solving and innovation.

Limited Candidate Pool

Finding diverse candidates can be challenging in certain geographic areas:

- Expand your search geographically by considering remote work options
- Develop internship or apprenticeship programs to nurture diverse talent

- Partner with local educational institutions to build a candidate pipeline
- Create fellowship programs to attract emerging professionals from diverse backgrounds
- Consider candidates with skill-adjacent career paths, such as journalism, macro-social work, and business development, just to name a few

Retention Difficulties

Once you've recruited diverse team members, keeping them engaged is crucial:

- Conduct regular check-ins to address concerns proactively
- Ensure equitable compensation and growth opportunities
- Create affinity groups or mentorship programs to support underrepresented staff
- Celebrate contributions from all team members, not just the most visible
- Provide ongoing DEI education to create an organization-wide culture of inclusion
- Share organizational goals and progress openly, inviting input from all
- Address microaggressions and exclusionary behaviors immediately

Reflection Question

- What's your organization's biggest challenge in building a diverse team?
- Brainstorm three potential solutions, no matter how unconventional.

Ethical Considerations in Diversity Initiatives

As we strive to build diverse teams, it's crucial to consider the ethical implications of our efforts:

Avoiding Tokenism

- Ensure diverse team members are valued for their skills and contributions, not just their demographic representation

- Create meaningful opportunities for leadership and decision-making
- Avoid overburdening underrepresented team members with diversity-related tasks

Balancing Merit and Diversity

- Develop clear, objective criteria for hiring and promotion
- Implement blind review processes where possible
- Provide equal access to professional development opportunities

Addressing Power Dynamics

- Recognize and address existing power structures that may disadvantage certain groups
- Create safe channels for reporting discrimination or unfair treatment
- Ensure leadership is accountable for fostering an inclusive environment

Power dynamics are such a pervasive issue in our sector that we've devoted Chapter 8, "Navigating Power Dynamics in Human-Centered Fundraising," to the topic.

Data Privacy and Consent

- Be transparent about how diversity data will be collected and used
- Allow team members to self-identify their diverse attributes rather than making assumptions
- Protect sensitive information and respect individual privacy preferences

Reflection Question

How can your organization ensure its diversity initiatives are ethical and respectful of all individuals involved?

Small Organization Spotlight: Diversity on a Budget

Even with limited resources, small nonprofits can make significant strides in building diverse teams:

Leverage Volunteer Power

- Create diverse volunteer committees to support recruitment efforts
- Offer skill-building opportunities that can lead to paid positions

Embrace Remote Work

- Expand your talent pool by offering remote or hybrid positions
- Use free or low-cost virtual collaboration tools to support distributed teams

Partner for Progress

- Form alliances with other small nonprofits to share resources and best practices
- Collaborate on joint training initiatives or mentorship programs

Start Small, Think Big

- Focus on one key diversity goal at a time
- Celebrate small wins to build momentum and support for larger initiatives

Reflection Question

If you're part of a small nonprofit, which of these strategies could you implement immediately to increase diversity without straining your budget?

The Future of Diverse Fundraising

As we look ahead, diversity in fundraising teams will become increasingly crucial. The landscape is evolving rapidly, presenting both exciting opportunities and notable challenges for nonprofit organizations. Here's a deeper dive into what the future holds:

Shifting Donor Demographics

In the upcoming years, we'll see a significant shift in donor demographics. As a result of the ongoing US generational transfer of wealth, Millennials and Gen Z will comprise a larger portion of the donor base, bringing with them new expectations and giving behaviors. These younger donors prioritize:

- Social impact and transparency
- Digital-first engagement
- Frequent, smaller donations over large, occasional gifts
- Alignment with personal values and causes

To adapt, fundraising teams will need to:

- Develop robust digital strategies, including mobile-friendly platforms and social media campaigns
- Create more engaging, interactive fundraising events and experiences that appeal to younger audiences
- Provide detailed impact reports and real-time updates on how donations are used

Technology-Driven Personalization

Artificial intelligence and data analytics are revolutionizing donor engagement. So much so that we've devoted Chapter 10, "AI: The Responsible and Beneficial Sidekick in Human-Centered Fundraising," to it.

Fundraising teams will leverage technological tools to:

- Create hyper-personalized outreach strategies
- Predict donor behavior and giving potential more accurately
- Automate routine tasks, freeing up time for relationship-building

However, this technological shift will also present challenges:

- Ensuring data privacy and ethical use of donor information
- Maintaining a human touch in increasingly automated processes
- Training staff to effectively use new technologies

Diverse Funding Sources

The competition for traditional funding sources will intensify, pushing nonprofits to diversify their revenue streams. We can expect to see:

- Increased focus on monthly giving programs and subscription-based donations
- Growth in peer-to-peer and social fundraising campaigns
- More nonprofits exploring social enterprise models and earned income strategies

Challenges will include:

- Developing the skills to manage multiple revenue streams effectively
- Balancing mission-driven work with potential commercial activities
- Navigating complex regulatory environments for diverse funding models

Global and Virtual Engagement

In the coming years, geographic boundaries will continue to matter less in fundraising. We'll see:

- More nonprofits engaging international donors
- Increased use of virtual and augmented reality for immersive donor experiences
- Growth in global peer-to-peer fundraising networks

This global shift will require:

- Cultural competence and language skills within fundraising teams
- Understanding of international giving laws and regulations
- Investment in secure, global payment processing systems

Emphasis on Equity and Inclusion

Diverse fundraising teams will become increasingly essential not only for representation but also for organizational success. We can expect the following:

- The continued reduction of federal and state funding for human services, education, and healthcare
- Donors increasingly consider an organization's commitment to diversity when deciding to give
- More foundations and non-government grants require evidence of diverse leadership and inclusive practices
- Emergence of new private funding opportunities specifically supporting minority-led nonprofits

Challenges will include:

- Addressing systemic barriers to diversity in nonprofit leadership
- Developing inclusive cultures that retain diverse talent
- Balancing the need for experienced fundraisers with the drive for fresh, diverse perspectives

Climate Change and Sustainability

Environmental concerns will significantly impact fundraising in the coming years:

- Increased donor interest in climate-related causes
- Growing expectation for nonprofits to demonstrate sustainable practices
- Potential for new "green" fundraising methods and carbon-neutral campaigns

Fundraising teams will need to:

- Develop expertise in environmental issues and sustainability practices
- Adapt events and operations to minimize environmental impact
- Create compelling narratives linking their cause to broader environmental concerns

As we navigate these emerging trends, diverse fundraising teams will be uniquely positioned to innovate, adapt, and thrive. By embracing diversity now, organizations lay the groundwork for resilience and success in the dynamic fundraising landscape of the years to come.

Key Takeaways and Action Steps

Key Takeaways

- **Diversity is a Superpower:** Building a diverse fundraising team means bringing together individuals with distinct strengths—cultural intelligence, innovation, community relationships, and specialized skills. Like assembling a league of superheroes, this diversity empowers organizations to approach challenges creatively and make greater impact.

- **Live Your Values:** For nonprofit organizations, equity and inclusion aren't just ideals—they're central to the mission. A diverse team signals authentic commitment to these values, internally and externally, and reinforces your nonprofit's credibility.

- **Get the Right People on the Bus:** Inspired by Jim Collins's principle in *Good to Great and the Social Sectors*, it's not enough to hire for diversity alone; you must also ensure each team member is in the role that taps into their unique abilities and passions.

- **Intentional Hiring Practices Matter:** Every touchpoint—especially job postings—communicates your organization's values. Explicitly state your commitment to inclusion and design a recruitment process that welcomes candidates from all backgrounds.

Action Steps

- **Audit and Articulate Your Values:** Regularly reaffirm your commitment to equity and inclusion, both in internal conversations and external messaging. Let these values shine through in everyday practice.

- **Craft Inclusive Job Postings:** Make your dedication to diversity and belonging unmistakable. Use inviting, bias-free language, and clearly outline your vision for an inclusive workplace.

- **Bias-Proof Your Hiring Process:** Re-examine your screening questions, evaluation criteria, and interview panels. Where possible, implement structured interviews and blind resume reviews to prioritize potential over pedigree.
- **Seek Out Superpowers:** When recruiting or promoting team members, look beyond traditional qualifications. Value lived experience and community ties just as highly as technical expertise.
- **Build Belonging:** Once your heroes join the team, foster an environment where everyone can thrive. Celebrate unique contributions, encourage open dialogue, and provide opportunities for all voices to be heard.
- **Ongoing Learning:** Stay open to feedback and continual improvement. Invest in equity and inclusion training and resources for your staff.

By assembling and empowering a truly diverse League of Heroes, your fundraising team can break barriers, unlock new opportunities, and create a lasting positive impact.

Diversity as a Pathway to Unity and Collective Impact

Diversity is not just an end goal; it is the foundation upon which unity and collective impact are built. While diversity brings fresh perspectives, innovative ideas, and authentic connections to your organization, its true potential is realized when these varied voices align around shared goals.

Building a diverse team is just the beginning of your organization's transformation. The real magic happens when these diverse individuals come together as a cohesive force with board members, volunteers, program participants, community partners, and other departments in your organization. We'll explore that in our next chapter as the "League of Heroes" paradigm.

Think about your favorite superhero teams: each member brings unique powers, perspectives, and skills, yet they're united by a common purpose. Similarly, your diverse fundraising team members each bring their own "superpowers" to the table. When these powers are recognized, respected, and strategically deployed, your team becomes greater than the sum of its parts.

The diverse team you're assembling isn't just about representation—it's about creating the foundation for a powerful collaborative approach that will transform your fundraising results and organizational impact. As we transition from focusing on building diversity to leveraging it through unity, you'll discover practical strategies for assembling and empowering your own League of Heroes.

Think of diversity as the rich palette of colors that make up a masterpiece—each hue is unique and essential, but it's their harmony that creates a work of art. For example, a diverse fundraising team might include individuals with expertise in major donor cultivation, grassroots organizing, social media strategy, and community engagement. Each member brings unique strengths to the table, but without collaboration and alignment, their efforts could remain fragmented. Unity ensures these diverse talents work together seamlessly, amplifying their collective impact.

This alignment doesn't happen by chance—it requires intentionality. As nonprofit leaders, we must create environments where diverse perspectives are not only welcomed but also integrated into decision-making processes. By fostering trust, encouraging collaboration, and aligning around a shared mission, we can transform a group of individuals into a cohesive force for change.

In the next chapter, we'll explore how this transformation unfolds through the League of Heroes paradigm. This approach takes the principles of diversity discussed here and elevates them into a model of collaborative heroism—where every individual's unique "superpower" contributes to extraordinary outcomes.

Final Reflection: As you prepare to dive into the next chapter, take a moment to envision your ideal "League of Heroes." What unique strengths would each team member bring? How would they work together to achieve extraordinary results? Let this vision inspire you as we explore the power of unity in diversity.

Building a diverse fundraising team isn't about meeting perfunctory quotas—it's about assembling a group with complementary strengths, each bringing unique perspectives to your mission. By embracing diversity, you're transforming your organization's potential for impact. Every step toward greater diversity advances you toward a more vibrant, effective, and successful fundraising future. Your mission deserves nothing less than a team of diverse heroes working together to change the world.

Remember that diversity is both a journey and a destination. The process of building and nurturing a diverse team will strengthen your organization even as you work toward your goals. The insights and relationships you develop along the way will enrich your fundraising practice and deepen your impact.

Are you ready to assemble your team of heroes? In the next chapter, we'll explore how to unite these diverse individuals into a cohesive, unstoppable force for good. Get ready to unlock the full potential of your League of Heroes.

6 | The League of Heroes Paradigm: Unity in Diversity

"We have no hope of solving our problems without harnessing
the diversity, the energy, and the creativity of all our people."
—Roger Wilkins, American Lawyer and Civil Rights Leader

A diverse team is a powerful asset, but its true potential is realized only when those differences are harnessed in pursuit of a common goal. Diversity alone is not enough; unity and collaboration are essential to achieving extraordinary results.

Building on the foundation laid in Chapter 5, this chapter explores how to unite your diverse team into a cohesive force for change—a League of Heroes. While diversity brings fresh perspectives and innovative ideas, unity ensures these perspectives align toward common goals. This chapter introduces the League of Heroes paradigm, where every stakeholder—board members, staff, volunteers, donors, program participants, and community partners—becomes part of a collaborative effort that drives extraordinary results.

We'll dive into strategies for fostering collaboration, managing team dynamics, and measuring collective impact. By the end of this chapter, you'll have practical tools to transform your diverse team into a unified league capable of achieving remarkable outcomes.

From Diversity to Unity

As I stood before a room full of passionate nonprofit professionals at a recent conference, I couldn't help but smile. The energy was palpable, each person radiating with the desire to make a difference. But as I listened to their stories, a common thread emerged: many felt isolated in their efforts, like solo crusaders fighting an uphill battle and feeling misunderstood.

That's when it hit me. In our quest to change the world, we often celebrate individual heroes—the major donor who writes a transformative check, the charismatic leader who inspires others to give, the courageous program participants who achieved a transformational milestone, the tireless volunteer and community leader who goes above and beyond, *and on rare occasions*—we even celebrate devoted staff. While these contributions all matter deeply, I've come to realize that the most powerful force for change emerges when we unite our diverse strengths and perspectives. And when we unite around a common purpose, we not only accomplish more, we feel less alone.

Welcome to the League of Heroes paradigm, where collective heroism drives extraordinary fundraising success. In this chapter, we'll explore how to assemble your own league, harnessing the unique superpowers of everyone involved in your mission—from board members and volunteers, program participants, to donors and community members, as well as staff. We'll dive into strategies for fostering collaboration, managing team dynamics, and measuring collective impact. Along the way, we'll encounter real-world examples of organizations that have successfully implemented this approach, and we'll tackle common challenges head-on.

So, fellow nonprofit heroes, are you ready to unlock the full potential of your organization's diverse superpowers? Let's embark on this heroic journey together.

Reflection Questions

Think about your organization.

- Who are the unsung heroes that contribute to your mission in ways that might not be immediately obvious?
- How could recognizing and leveraging their unique strengths enhance your collective impact?

The Power of Collaborative Heroism

Imagine a world where everyone involved in your nonprofit's mission sees themselves as an integral part of a heroic team. This is the essence of the League of Heroes approach. By fostering collaboration and mutual empowerment—by creating a sense of belonging—we achieve far more than any single hero could alone.

I worked with a nonprofit dedicated to providing healthcare and health education to underserved communities. They were struggling with siloed departments and a disconnect between their donors and the communities they served. You might be able to relate. I'm here to show you, it's not hopeless as you'll see throughout this chapter, their transformation into a true League of Heroes revolutionized their impact and fundraising success.

To illustrate the power of collaborative heroism, let's look at a real-world example that beautifully embodies this concept.

Case Study: The League of Heroes World Cup

Picture this: veterans from eight nations coming together not on a battlefield but on a soccer field. This is the inaugural League of Heroes World Cup, an innovative fundraising initiative aimed at raising funds and awareness for veterans experiencing homelessness.

What makes this campaign remarkable is how it unites diverse stakeholders:

- **Veterans:** As players from eight nations, they become the face of the campaign, sharing their stories and inspiring others.

- **Volunteers:** A dedicated team manages logistics, coordinates events, and spreads the word.
- **Donors:** From small individual contributions to corporate sponsorships, donors at all levels play crucial roles.
- **Community Partners:** Local businesses and organizations provide support through sponsorships, in-kind donations, and promotional assistance.
- **Staff:** Providing oversight and guidance, orchestrating all the moving parts of this event from pre-planning *(project plan, budget, volunteer recruitment, marketing, etc.)* to event day management and post-event stewardship activities.
- **Founder:** Jono Farrelly cares deeply about homeless veterans due to his personal experiences and understanding of the challenges they face. He tells stories about the difficulties he encountered adjusting to civilian life after leaving the military, which included periods of homelessness.

The result? A community event that brings all of their constituents together to increase financial support for veterans experiencing homelessness while building lasting connections and raising awareness of an important issue. This exemplifies the League of Heroes paradigm—diverse individuals and groups with shared values come together, each contributing their unique "superpower" to create something extraordinary.

Reflection Questions

- How could your organization create a signature event or initiative that brings together diverse stakeholders, each contributing their unique strengths?
- How could you convene a diverse group of stakeholders to create an online peer-to-peer campaign or help streamline an intake process, prohibiting prospective clients from gaining access to programs?
- What might be the potential impact of such an initiative?

Building Your League: Strategies for Unity in Diversity

Now that we've seen an example of the League of Heroes approach, let's explore how to implement this paradigm in your organization. This approach is about fostering unity and innovation through diverse perspectives, constructive criticism, and even dissent. It's about paying attention to what truly matters, especially during turbulent times when it's easy to overlook what drives meaningful change.

Here are four key strategies that I've seen work wonders in nonprofits of all sizes and missions.

Identify and Convene Your Diverse League of Heroes

Every person possesses unique strengths, influence, skills, and insights from their lived experiences. The first step in building your League of Heroes is identifying and celebrating these lived experiences and the diverse abilities of people within your various constituent groups. This includes program participants, community partners, volunteers, board members, donors, and staff.

Foster Cross-Functional Collaboration

Silos are the kryptonite of collective heroism. To ensure the greatest good, we must break down barriers between teams, departments, and even board committees to encourage creative collaboration. Intentionally curating cross-functional teams that challenge assumptions, spark innovation, and prevent stagnation in decision-making. This helps ensure organizations don't fall into the trap of the echo chamber, where everyone seemingly agrees and innovation is stifled.

As an example, a client who leads philanthropy efforts for an education and healthcare organization made a practice of attending team meetings of other departments: Primary Care, Behavioral Healthcare, and Surgical Services. In those meetings, she learned of the need for advanced medical equipment and ongoing healthcare team training, as well as the health equity challenges facing some neighborhoods in the greater community. That increased understanding and collaboration resulted in major donor and institutional investment opportunities, impact statements for direct response appeals, and more. Likewise, the physicians, clinicians, and nurses gained a newfound respect for their philanthropy colleagues and a deeper understanding of fundraising. It seems we fundraisers do more than throw great parties, after all!

The American Red Cross provides an excellent example of this strategy in action. In disaster recovery efforts, the Red Cross partners with organizations like Team Rubicon to address specific needs efficiently. For example, Stephanie Munoz, a Red Cross disaster program manager, collaborated with Team Rubicon on wildfire recovery projects in Colorado. She cross-trained in skills like chainsaw operation while providing CPR and emergency training to Team Rubicon volunteers. This partnership allowed both organizations to share expertise, recruit volunteers, and fill gaps in disaster response capabilities.

Invite Active Participation in Your Mission

Move beyond the traditional donor-recipient dynamic. Invite donors to be active participants in your mission, contributing not just money but also ideas, skills, and connections. Now, let me be clear: we invite our donors and others to share their ideas. That does not mean we are obligated to implement every idea. Doing so would further fuel the power dynamics issue that plagues the sector. Rather, we explore ideas and opportunities without attachment to them. You'll learn more about power dynamics in Chapter 8, "Navigating Power Dynamics in Human-Centered Fundraising."

But before donors, board members, volunteers, and staff can truly be effective in participating in your mission, they need to be prepped for success. That means participating in DEI *(Diversity, Equity, and Inclusion)* training. DEI training is a structured program designed to foster an inclusive and equitable engagement by helping employees, volunteers, and donors understand the importance of embracing diversity, promoting fairness, and creating an environment where everyone feels safe, valued, and respected. While the US government, under the administration of President Donald Trump, has taken significant steps to dismantle Diversity, Equity, and Inclusion (DEI) initiatives within the federal government, we must hold ourselves to a higher standard.

One client took this approach to heart by creating a "Skills Bank," where constituents could offer their professional expertise. This led to a pro bono legal clinic for community members and a donor-led workshop series on financial literacy. Another client engaged constituents with skilled trades expertise to join corporate volunteers in a campus beautification project each Spring and again in the Fall. Not only did this deepen community engagement, but it also significantly expanded the organization's capacity to serve its community.

Ensure the Communities You Serve Are Central to Program Planning and Decision-Making

To truly embody the League of Heroes paradigm, ensure that the communities you serve are central to your planning and decision-making processes. Who better to inform program planning and decision-making than those with lived experience related to your cause and in the community you serve? Programs developed with program participant collaboration are stronger than programs without community voice.

The Harlem Children's Zone provides an inspiring example of this approach. They practice community-centered design by employing local residents as "Block Captains" who provide insights into community needs and help shape program delivery. This ensures that their initiatives are truly responsive to the community's needs and aspirations.

Reflection Questions

- Which of these four strategies resonates most with your organization's current needs?
- What's one concrete step you could take in the next week to start implementing this strategy?

Managing Team Dynamics in Your League of Heroes

As we assemble our diverse team of heroes, it's crucial to address the challenges that can arise when different personalities and work styles come together. In my experience, managing these dynamics effectively is key to maintaining a cohesive League of Heroes.

Understanding Different Working Styles

Just as superheroes have different powers and approaches, your team members have diverse working preferences and communication styles. Recognizing and accommodating these differences can significantly enhance collaboration.

This approach is embraced by organizations like The Nature Conservancy. They use the DiSC assessment tool to help their diverse teams understand each other's communication preferences and work styles, leading to more effective collaboration across their global organization. They've seen a 30% reduction in project delays after implementing this approach.

Adopting the Principles of Constructive Conflict

Constructive conflict involves addressing disagreements in a way that fosters collaboration, creativity, and positive outcomes. Instead of avoiding conflict, it embraces differences as opportunities for growth. Below are the key principles that underpin constructive conflict resolution:

1. **Open Communication:** Encouraging transparent and honest dialogue is essential for resolving conflicts constructively. This involves creating an environment where individuals feel safe to express their thoughts and concerns without fear of judgment or retaliation.

2. **Active Listening:** Listening attentively to understand the perspectives, needs, and motivations of all parties involved is crucial. Active listening promotes empathy and helps uncover the root causes of conflict, paving the way for mutually beneficial solutions.

3. **Respectful Dialogue:** Respect is a cornerstone of constructive conflict. Participants should engage in discussions with civility, valuing each other's viewpoints even when disagreements arise. This fosters trust and psychological safety within teams or relationships.

4. **Focus on Solutions:** Constructive conflict prioritizes finding actionable solutions rather than dwelling on problems or assigning blame. It seeks outcomes that address the needs of all parties involved, often through collaborative problem-solving techniques like brainstorming or consensus-building.

5. **Encouragement of Diverse Perspectives:** Constructive conflict values differing opinions and encourages their expression. By welcoming diverse viewpoints, teams can arrive at more informed decisions and innovative solutions.

6. **Emotional Regulation:** Managing emotions constructively ensures that discussions remain productive and do not escalate into personal attacks or destructive behaviors. Balanced emotional dynamics help maintain focus on resolving the issue at hand.

7. **Learning and Growth Mindset:** Viewing conflicts as opportunities for learning reframes them as valuable experiences rather than obstacles. This mindset fosters resilience and adaptability, encouraging participants to grow from challenges.

8. **Clear Guidelines:** Establishing ground rules for addressing conflicts can help structure discussions and prevent escalation. Guidelines may include protocols for raising concerns, facilitating dialogue, and reaching resolutions.

9. **Constructive Feedback:** A culture of constructive feedback allows individuals to share insights in a non-confrontational manner, using structured approaches like the SBI (Situation-Behavior-Impact) method to address issues effectively.

10. **Collaboration Over Competition:** Rather than approaching conflicts with a win-lose mentality, constructive conflict emphasizes collaboration to achieve win-win outcomes that benefit all parties involved.

By adhering to these principles, individuals and organizations can transform conflicts into opportunities for innovation, strengthened relationships, and improved decision-making processes.

Navigating Conflict Constructively

Even the most aligned heroes occasionally clash at times. Establishing healthy conflict resolution processes is crucial for maintaining a strong League.

Doctors Without Borders provides an excellent example of this in action. They implement a "Constructive Conflict" framework that helps their diverse international teams address disagreements while maintaining respect and focus on their shared mission. This approach has been particularly effective in high-stress field operations where quick decisions must be made by teams from different cultural backgrounds.

Ensuring Equitable Recognition

In a collaborative model, it can be challenging to ensure that all contributions are equitably recognized and valued, especially when some roles are more visible than others.

The nonprofit GlobalGiving tackled this challenge head-on by creating a "Contribution Mapping" tool. This innovative approach visualizes how different team members' efforts connect to successful outcomes, ensuring that both front-line and behind-the-scenes heroes receive appropriate recognition for their role in mission achievements.

Reflection Question

Think about a recent conflict or misunderstanding within your team.

- How could the principles of constructive conflict resolution have helped navigate that situation more effectively?

Leveraging Technology to Empower Your League of Heroes

In today's digital age, technology plays a crucial role in enabling and enhancing collaboration within your League of Heroes. Let's explore how various tools and platforms can support your collaborative efforts:

Project Management and Collaboration Platforms

Cloud-based tools like Asana, Trello, or Monday.com can help your team stay organized and aligned on projects and tasks from anywhere with an internet connection. These platforms allow you to:

- Assign tasks and track progress
- Share files and collaborate on documents
- Set deadlines and reminders
- Visualize project timelines and workflows

For example, Hopeful Horizons uses Asana to manage their cross-departmental initiatives, allowing team members from different departments to easily collaborate and stay updated on project progress.

Communication Tools

Platforms like Slack, Microsoft Teams, or Zoom can facilitate real-time communication and foster a sense of connection among team members, especially in remote or hybrid work environments.

These tools offer:

- Instant messaging and group chats
- Video conferencing capabilities
- File sharing and searchable message history
- Integration with other productivity tools
- AI note-taking features and plug-ins

The American Red Cross uses Slack to connect its diverse teams across different locations, creating dedicated channels for various projects and initiatives.

Virtual Collaboration Spaces

Tools like Miro or MURAL provide virtual whiteboards and collaboration spaces that can be particularly useful for brainstorming sessions, strategic planning, and visual project mapping.

These platforms allow teams to:

- Collaborate in real-time on visual boards
- Use templates for various collaboration exercises
- Integrate with other tools like video conferencing platforms

Doctors Without Borders uses Miro for their strategic planning sessions, allowing team members from different countries to contribute ideas and visualize complex projects together.

Donor and Volunteer Management Systems

Specialized software like Salesforce Nonprofit Cloud, Bloomerang, or DonorPerfect can help you manage relationships with your donors and volunteers more effectively. These systems can:

- Track donor interactions and giving history
- Manage volunteer schedules and skills

- Generate reports on fundraising and engagement metrics
- Integrate with other tools like email marketing platforms

GlobalGiving uses Salesforce Nonprofit Cloud to manage their donor relationships and track the impact of various projects, allowing them to provide detailed updates to their supporters.

Learning Management Systems

Platforms like TalentLMS or Docebo can help you provide ongoing training and development opportunities for your team, volunteers, and even donors. An LMS can:

- Host online courses and training materials
- Track learning progress and certifications
- Facilitate peer-to-peer learning and knowledge sharing

The Nature Conservancy uses an LMS to provide ongoing training to their global workforce, ensuring that all team members have access to the latest best practices and organizational knowledge.

By strategically implementing these technologies, you can enhance collaboration, streamline processes, and ultimately amplify the impact your League of Heroes has on the communities you serve.

Reflection Questions

- Which area of your organization's operations could benefit most from improved technological support?
- What's one tool or platform you could explore to address this need?

Storytelling: The Superpower That Unites Us All

At the heart of every great team of heroes is a compelling narrative that binds them together. In the nonprofit world, storytelling is the superpower that unites diverse stakeholders around a common cause. Chapter 7, "Crafting the Narrative: Storytelling in Human-Centered Fundraising," is devoted to storytelling. But for now, let's focus on storytelling as a tool for attracting and retaining your League of Heroes.

People long to be part of something bigger than themselves. Your organization can help fulfill that desire. But first, we need to capture their attention, hearts, and minds.

Craft a Unifying Origin Story

Every League of Heroes needs an origin story. For your nonprofit, this means articulating your founding mission in a way that resonates with all stakeholders.

Civilla's origin story begins, "Before we started Civilla, one of our co-founders, Mike, spent six years carrying around a 40+ page scroll in his back pocket. No, it wasn't a medieval artifact or a Shakespearean sonnet (though it was longer than Macbeth). It was the 1,000-question, 18,000-word application for public benefits in the state of Michigan."

Formally known as the DHS-1171, the application was the longest of its kind in America at over 40 pages—a formidable barrier for over 2.5 million residents each year.

Mike had come across the application in his previous work with the United Way and had kept it in his back pocket, quite literally, ever since. It served as a daily reminder of how public institutions, originally designed to serve residents and communities, so often stray from that purpose. It also served as inspiration—pointing to the potential that human-centered design could unlock for these organizations.

Human-centered design is a process that aims to solve problems by deeply understanding the experiences of the people who are most affected by them. From there, solutions can be built that meet real needs. To kick off every project, Civilla begins with user research to build an understanding of people's experiences. The Michigan public benefits application was no exception.

Civilla spent hours at kitchen tables and in living rooms, working to understand the public benefits through the eyes of those who interacted with the system every day. Residents shared their perspectives on problems with the system, and what they hoped it could look like instead. Civilla researchers heard that people felt lost. They didn't know how to navigate the process, who to ask for help, or what came next. They heard people describe feeling like "a number in a mechanical system" rather than humans with complex stories to tell.

Likewise, they heard frustration from Michigan Department of Health and Human Services (MDHHS) employees who felt stuck between wanting to help people and broken legacy systems.

Civilla is a nonprofit design studio working to create a more beautiful civil society by orienting public institutions around people.

This origin story not only explains the organization's purpose but also invites everyone to view the residents applying for public benefits and MDHHS employees with a deeper understanding and empathy.

Highlight Individual and Collective Heroism

Share stories that demonstrate how individual contributions combine to create significant impact. This approach validates each person's role while emphasizing the power of teamwork. Seeing others joining together for a purpose.

Create a Shared Language of Heroism

Develop vocabulary that reinforces the League of Heroes concept and makes everyone feel part of something bigger than themselves.

At Stand Together, they use the following language:

- Instead of "donors," the organization describes its donors and partners as "Changemakers" and emphasizes collaboration with a diverse range of individuals, including business leaders, philanthropists, and social entrepreneurs.
- Stand Together emphasizes that *every person* has unique gifts and potential, and their work aims to empower individuals to realize this potential and contribute positively to society.
- Stand Together's vision is to create a society where everyone can live a life of meaning and succeed by benefiting others. They focus on transforming key institutions like education, business, communities, and government to empower people from the bottom up.

By consistently using this language in their communications, they reinforce that everyone involved is a crucial part of their heroic mission.

Integrate Stories with Data

The most powerful nonprofit narratives combine emotional stories with concrete data about impact, creating a complete picture of how your League of Heroes makes a difference. Humans are emotional beings. The data, albeit brief, helps us rationalize our emotional decision to give.

Charity: Water is a nonprofit organization that masterfully combines the personal stories of water recipients with precise data about well locations, costs, and impact. They tell these stories in an inspiring, strength-based manner. Their interactive maps connect donor contributions directly to specific communities, creating a transparent narrative about collective impact.

Overcoming Challenges: When Heroes Face Obstacles

Even the mightiest heroes face challenges, and implementing the League of Heroes paradigm is no exception. Let's address some common obstacles you will likely encounter and how to overcome them.

Challenge 1: Resistance to Change

Some team members or long-time donors may prefer traditional hierarchies or individual recognition.

Solution: Start small and lead by example. Implement the League of Heroes approach in a specific project, demonstrating its effectiveness before rolling it out organization-wide. Share success stories from those who have embraced the new paradigm.

When Hopeful Horizons initially faced pushback in involving donors in program design, we started with a pilot project. They invited a small group of engaged donors to participate in a workshop alongside staff and community members. The success of this initiative, which led to a new mentorship program, helped convince skeptics of the value of collaboration.

Challenge 2: Balancing Different Perspectives

With diverse stakeholders comes a diversity of opinions, which can sometimes lead to conflicts.

Solution: Establish clear processes for collaborative decision-making. This might include consensus-building techniques or implementing a system where different stakeholder groups have representation in key decisions.

The Environmental Defense Fund uses a "Solutions Mapping" technique in their collaborative projects. This approach visually maps out different stakeholder perspectives and potential solutions, helping teams find common ground and innovative compromises.

Challenge 3: Maintaining Long-Term Engagement

Initial enthusiasm for the League of Heroes concept may wane over time if not consistently reinforced.

Solution: Create ongoing opportunities for collaboration and recognition through regular features in your newsletter, annual awards ceremonies, or mentorship programs pairing experienced "heroes" with newcomers.

At Hopeful Horizons, they implemented a quarterly "League of Heroes Summit," bringing together staff, volunteers, donors, and community members for a day of shared learning, problem-solving, and celebration. This regular event helps maintain enthusiasm and reinforces the collaborative culture.

Another organization simply pulled the "Heroes" theme into their annual volunteer recognition luncheon, ensuring every constituent group had meaningful engagement and representation.

Challenge 4: Resource Limitations

Smaller organizations may worry they lack the capacity to implement a comprehensive League of Heroes approach.

Solution: Scale the implementation to fit your organization's size and resources. Even small organizations can begin with basic collaborative practices and expand over time.

I once worked with a community-based literacy nonprofit with just three staff members. We created a monthly "Heroes Huddle" potluck dinner where volunteers, donors, and community members could connect informally. This low-cost initiative fostered collaboration that led to new program ideas and increased volunteer retention by 40%.

The League of Heroes in the Current Nonprofit Landscape

As we implement the League of Heroes paradigm, it's crucial to consider how this approach intersects with current trends in the nonprofit sector. Let's explore how some of these trends can enhance our collaborative approach.

Digital Transformation

The rapid digitalization of the nonprofit sector offers new opportunities for collaboration and engagement within our League of Heroes. But we must not assume every League of Heroes member has reliable and consistent access to technology.

Hopeful Horizons leveraged digital tools to create a virtual "Hero Hub," an online platform where staff, volunteers, donors, and community members could connect, share ideas, and collaborate on projects in real time. This digital space became particularly valuable during the COVID-19 pandemic, allowing the League of Heroes to remain active and engaged despite physical distancing measures.

Impact Investing and Collaborative Funding

The growing trend of impact investing and collaborative funding models aligns perfectly with the League of Heroes paradigm.

The Rockefeller Foundation's Zero Gap Fund brings together diverse stakeholders—including investors, entrepreneurs, and nonprofits—to develop innovative financing solutions for global challenges. This collaborative approach embodies the League of Heroes spirit, leveraging diverse expertise to create systemic change.

Rise of Social Enterprises

Social enterprises, which blend business models with social impact, offer new opportunities for cross-sector collaboration within our League of Heroes.

Feeding America partnered with several food-based social enterprises to create the "MealConnect" platform, which enables the recovery and redistribution of surplus food. This collaborative initiative brings together nonprofits, businesses, and volunteers in a unified system that reduces food waste while addressing hunger.

Diversity, Equity, and Inclusion

The nonprofit sector's increased focus on diversity, equity, and inclusion (DEI) resonates strongly with the League of Heroes paradigm's emphasis on unity in diversity. Despite the US federal government's recent actions to dismantle DEI initiatives under President Trump, those values can continue to thrive without federal support if we join together in the community.

An example of a federal initiative being dismantled yet continuing to thrive in communities is the Trump administration's efforts to eliminate the Institute of Museum and Library Services (IMLS) through an executive order issued on March 14, 2025. The IMLS was the primary federal agency supporting libraries and museums across the United States, providing grants for literacy programs, workforce development, technology upgrades, and cultural preservation projects. Despite its elimination at the federal level, libraries and museums have continued to serve as vital community hubs through state and local efforts, leveraging partnerships and community-driven initiatives to sustain their programs.

The Sierra Club reformed its leadership structure to ensure that front-line communities most affected by environmental issues have direct representation in strategic decisions. This shift has led to more effective programs and a more diverse supporter base.

Measuring Success: KPIs for Your League of Heroes

To ensure the effectiveness of your League of Heroes approach, it's crucial to establish clear key performance indicators (KPIs). Here are specific metrics I recommend considering:

Collaboration Index

Measure the frequency, quality, and outcomes of collaborative efforts across your organization.

Specific metrics:
- Number of cross-departmental projects completed
- Percentage of initiatives involving multiple stakeholder groups
- Constituent assessment scores on cross-team collaboration
- Time from idea generation to implementation for collaborative projects

Tools for measurement: Project management software, collaboration surveys, process timeline tracking.

Diversity of Contributions

Monitor the range of contributions beyond financial support.

Specific metrics:
- Number of skills-based volunteer hours
- Quantity and quality of pro bono professional services
- In-kind resource contributions
- Network expansion through stakeholder connections

Tools for measurement: Volunteer management systems, contribution tracking databases, and social network analysis.

Impact Multiplier

Assess how collaborative efforts amplify your organization's impact compared to prior siloed approaches.

Specific metrics:
- Program reach before and after implementing collaborative approaches
- Cost per beneficiary in collaborative vs. traditional programs
- Resource efficiency through shared capabilities
- Secondary impact through partnership ripple effects

Tools for measurement: Program evaluation systems, financial analysis tools, and partnership impact assessments.

Regularly gauge how fulfilled and valued your League of Heroes members feel.

Specific metrics:

- Team member satisfaction survey scores
- Qualitative feedback on collaborative experiences
- Stories of meaningful participation and connection

Tools for measurement: Pulse surveys, annual stakeholder assessments, focus groups, and story collection.

Reflection Question: Looking at these KPIs, which one do you think would be most revealing about the state of collaboration in your organization? Why?

Connecting Measurement to Action

The true value of these metrics comes from using them to continuously improve your League of Heroes approach.

Real-world example: The nonprofit GiveDirectly created a "Collaborative Impact Dashboard" that tracks metrics across all of the KPI areas. They review this dashboard quarterly with representatives from all stakeholder groups, using the data to identify both successes to celebrate and areas needing attention. This transparent approach to measurement has strengthened their collaborative culture and improved outcomes in their cash transfer programs.

By implementing these KPIs and regularly reviewing your progress, you'll be able to fine-tune your League of Heroes approach, ensuring that your collaborative efforts are truly driving greater impact and engagement across all stakeholder groups.

Final Reflection: As we transition to exploring the power of storytelling, take a moment to reflect on your organization's current narrative. Does it effectively capture the collaborative spirit of your League of Heroes? What elements might be missing, and how could a more inclusive story drive greater engagement and impact?

Key Takeaways and Action Steps

Key Takeaways

- **Unified Strength Outshines Solo Effort:** Diversity isn't just about bringing different perspectives to the table—it's about weaving those differences together into a united League of Heroes that achieves more than any individual could alone.
- **Collaboration Drives Impact:** True fundraising success happens when every stakeholder—board, staff, volunteers, donors, program participants, community partners—works collaboratively toward shared goals, not in silos.
- **Intentional Team Building:** Harnessing your organization's diverse talent means intentionally breaking down barriers between departments and involving all constituents in orientation, training, and communication.
- **The Power of Belonging:** When people move from feeling like isolated "crusaders" to active members of a collaborative league, morale soars, innovation flows, and impact multiplies.
- **Real-World Proof:** Transformational success stories prove that moving from siloed work to the League of Heroes model revolutionizes both community impact and fundraising outcomes.

Action Steps

- **Map Your League:** Identify every group that plays a role in your mission—board, staff, volunteers, donors, program participants, and community partners. Recognize each as a hero with unique strengths to contribute.
- **Foster Connection and Collaboration:** Hold regular cross-team meetings, shared trainings, and collaborative planning sessions. Ensure all stakeholders understand the big picture and how their efforts fit in.
- **Orient and Equip All Members:** Develop clear orientation processes and provide ongoing training so each "hero" knows not just their role—but how their contribution fits with others.

- **Break Down Silos:** Encourage open communication across departments and roles. Create systems for sharing successes, lessons learned, and feedback organization wide.
- **Measure and Celebrate Collective Impact:** Track not just individual or team achievements, but organization-wide progress. Celebrate "wins" that were made possible by everyone's combined effort.
- **Lead by Example:** Model unity, mutual respect, and openness to learning in your leadership style. When leaders champion collaboration, the league follows suit.

By moving your organization from diversity to unity, from solo efforts to collective heroism, you establish a League of Heroes that's equipped to achieve extraordinary fundraising goals—and change the world.

From Heroes to Storytellers: The Power of Narrative

As we conclude our exploration of the League of Heroes paradigm, it's important to recognize that every great team of champions is united by a compelling narrative. The stories we tell about our collective efforts have the power to inspire, motivate, and attract new heroes to our cause.

In Chapter 7, "Crafting the Narrative: Storytelling in Human-Centered Fundraising," we'll dive deep into the art of storytelling as a powerful tool for uniting your League of Heroes and inspiring action. We'll explore how to:

- Craft an overarching narrative that captures the essence of your collaborative efforts
- Highlight individual stories within the context of your collective impact
- Use storytelling to bridge the gap between donor-centric and community-centric approaches
- Leverage digital platforms to share your stories and engage a wider audience

By mastering the art of storytelling, you'll be able to:

1. Reinforce the shared purpose that unites your diverse League of Heroes
2. Inspire potential donors, volunteers, and partners to join your cause
3. Demonstrate the tangible impact of your collaborative efforts
4. Create emotional connections that drive long-term engagement and support

As you prepare to dive into the world of storytelling, consider this: How can the story of your League of Heroes inspire others to join your mission? What unique perspectives and experiences within your team could form the building blocks of a powerful narrative?

Remember, every hero in your league has a story to tell. By weaving these individual stories into a larger narrative of collective impact, you create a powerful force for change that resonates with supporters and beneficiaries alike.

7 | Crafting the Narrative: Storytelling in Human-Centered Fundraising

"When the storyteller tells the truth, she reminds us that human beings are more alike than unalike … A story is what it's like to be a human being—to be knocked down and to miraculously arise."

—Maya Angelou, Author and Civil Rights Activist

As I sat across from a dedicated volunteer at our local food bank, I couldn't help but be moved by the passion in her eyes as she recounted her experiences. "You know, Tammy," she said, leaning forward, "it's not just about filling empty stomachs. It's about restoring dignity, hope, and a sense of community." In that moment, I realized that she wasn't just telling me about her work; she was weaving a powerful narrative that encapsulated the very essence of our mission.

This, my fellow nonprofit heroes, is the magic of storytelling in fundraising. It's about more than just relaying facts and figures; it's about painting a vivid picture that connects hearts, ignites passions, and inspires action. In the world of nonprofit fundraising, stories are the secret sauce that can transform a simple ask into a compelling call to action and convey the impact of generosity in simple human terms.

As we dive into this chapter, I want you to think of yourself not just as a fundraiser but as a seasoned storyteller. Your mission? To craft narratives that bridge the gap between donors, volunteers, staff, program partners, and, of course, the communities we serve, creating a tapestry of shared purpose and mutual understanding. I want you to think of your program participants, volunteers, advocates, and donors as heroes—*every single one of them*. It's a tall order, I know, but fear not! I'm here to guide you through the art and science of storytelling in human-centered fundraising.

The Power of Storytelling in Human-Centered Fundraising

Picture this: You're at a cocktail party, and someone asks you what you do. You could rattle off statistics about your nonprofit's impact or worse—your organization's tax status, or you could tell them a story about a life changed because of your work. Which do you think would leave a lasting impression?

Humans are hardwired for stories. We use them to make sense of the world, to connect with others, and to find meaning in our experiences. In the context of human-centered fundraising, storytelling serves as a powerful tool to:

- **Create Emotional Connections:** Stories have the unique ability to evoke emotions and foster empathy. When donors hear about real-life experiences of individuals participating in your organization's work, they're more likely to feel a personal connection to your cause.
- **Bridge Perspectives:** By weaving together narratives that include both donor and community perspectives, you can create a sense of shared purpose. This approach honors the motivations of donors while centering the voices and experiences of those you serve.

- **Dispel Misconceptions and Stereotypes:** Ethical storytelling doesn't reinforce negative stereotypes or evoke feelings of sympathy. But rather, stories should be centered on empathy, dignity, and solidarity.
- **Illuminate the Complexities of the Challenges Your Organization Tackles:** Donors, volunteers, and community members want to understand the root causes of pervasive and systemic issues that plague our communities—and *what we're doing to mitigate them together.*
- **Convey Your Organization's Unique Value Proposition in the Community:** Why is your organization the one to address this issue? What's unique about your theory of change? How do you collaborate with mission-adjacent organizations to create comprehensive solutions?
- **Demonstrate Impact:** Stories provide concrete, relatable examples of how donations translate into real-world change. They bring your mission to life, showing donors the tangible results of their generosity. Showing volunteers and community members the impact of their time, energy, and leadership.
- **Create Opportunities:** Making space for program participants, volunteers, advocates, donors, and staff who choose to share their stories allows them to be generous and inspire others.
- **Inspire Action:** A well-crafted story can motivate your community to take action, whether that's making a donation, volunteering their time, becoming advocates for your cause—*or some combination.*
- **Build Trust and Authenticity:** Authentic storytelling demonstrates transparency and openness. It shows that your nonprofit isn't afraid to showcase your work, both the successes and the challenges.

Ethical and Empowering Storytelling

There's so much to say *(and continue learning)* about ethical and empowering storytelling. Regardless of whether stories are shared in print, video, or in person, they must be grounded in honesty and accuracy, ensuring that stories are represented truthfully without exaggeration or misrepresentation to maintain credibility. We must also obtain explicit written consent from individuals featured and portray them with dignity and respect, avoiding stereotypes or exploitation by using strength-based language. Providing sufficient context is essential to prevent misleading interpretations. Stories should aim to inform or inspire without causing harm, traumatizing the individuals featured or the story's listener, and avoiding the reinforcement of negative stereotypes. Transparency about the story's purpose and how the content will be used fosters trust, while empowering the individuals featured gives them agency over their narratives. Additionally, cultural sensitivity is crucial to respecting community differences and avoiding misrepresentation. Together, these elements help nonprofit organizations communicate effectively while upholding integrity and fostering trust. Ask yourself the question: If this were my story, how would I want it told? Even so, don't assume someone wants *their* story told in the same way you do. Always ask them!

Crafting Compelling Narratives: A Step-by-Step Guide

Now, let's roll up our sleeves and dive into the nitty-gritty of crafting compelling narratives. Think of this as your storytelling recipe—follow these steps, and you'll be whipping up irresistible narratives in no time!

- **Identify Your Core Message:** Before you start telling your story, you need to know what you're really trying to say. What's the heart of your mission? What problem are you solving? What makes your approach unique? For instance, if you're working on providing clean water in developing countries, your core message might be: "Access to clean water is a fundamental human right, and together, we can ensure that every community has this basic necessity."
- **Determine Your Desired Outcome:** What action do you want the story to inspire? Do you want the listener or the reader to give money or volunteer time? Do you want the listener or the reader to know the impact of their most recent gift? Are you seeking a thought partner by sharing a story about a challenge your organization is facing?
- **Choose Your Characters:** Every great story needs compelling characters. In your nonprofit narrative, consider including:
    - **Program Participants:** The individuals or communities who are directly impacted by your work.

- **Donors:** Supporters who have made a significant impact through their contributions of time, leadership, or financial investment.
- **Volunteers, Community Members, or Staff:** The unsung heroes on the front lines of your mission.

Remember, your characters should be in action or showing development. Your audience will connect with characters who are overcoming challenges, growing, or making a difference.

- **Set the Scene:** The setting of your story helps your audience visualize and connect with the narrative. While it's often natural to set your story around your organization's location, don't be afraid to mix things up. If you're raising funds for a new science lab, for instance, you might set scenes in your current laboratory, showcasing the limitations of the existing space and painting a picture of the possibilities a new facility could offer.
- **Develop Your Plot:** Every good story needs conflict and resolution. In your fundraising narrative:
  - **Conflict:** This is the problem your organization is trying to solve. For example, if you're fundraising for a college soccer team, showcase how lack of equipment or proper infrastructure has impacted them in the past.
  - **Resolution:** This is how your fundraising efforts can help solve the conflict. Are there any early actions being taken that you can highlight? Perhaps you could include a video where staff members are discussing plans to help the soccer team, showing potential donors that this is something in the works that they can help make a reality.
- **Use Emotional Language:** Facts and figures have their place, but emotions are what truly drive people to action. Use vivid language and sensory details to create a narrative that tugs at the heartstrings. Paint a picture that your donors can see, hear, and feel.
- **Showcase Your Impact:** People want to know that their contributions of time or money make a difference. Don't just tell them— show them! Share specific outcomes and success stories. Use data,

testimonials, and other evidence to demonstrate the effectiveness of your programs and services.

- **Make It Easy to Take Action:** Once you've captured your audience's attention with your story, make it easy for them to get involved. Include clear calls-to-action and donation links in your fundraising materials or sign-up links in your volunteer recruitment or community engagement promotions.

Real-World Examples: Storytelling Success Stories

Let's look at some real-world examples of nonprofits that have successfully used storytelling to bridge the gap between donor-centric and community-centric fundraising approaches:

Case Study: Charity:Water

Charity:Water, a nonprofit organization that provides clean and safe drinking water to people in developing countries, is a master class in storytelling for fundraising. Their approach:

- **Personal Stories:** They share stories of individuals whose lives have been transformed by access to clean water. These stories often include before-and-after narratives, showing the tangible impact of donations.
- **Donor Involvement:** Charity:Water involves donors in the storytelling process. They provide updates on specific projects that donors have funded, including GPS coordinates and joyful, strength-based photos of communities with completed wells.
- **Transparency:** They use storytelling to demonstrate transparency, showing exactly how donations are used and the impact they create.
- **Multimedia Approach:** Charity:Water uses a variety of media to tell their stories, including high-quality videos, photos, interactive web experiences and now, even a virtual reality, immersive in-person experience in Franklin, TN called The Experience Lab.

Result: This storytelling approach has helped Charity:Water raise millions of dollars and engage a large, loyal donor base. By connecting donors directly to the communities they're helping, they've created a powerful sense of involvement and impact.

Example: Project Renewal's Video Story

Video is one of the most effective tools for storytelling. With the right story angle, videos can evoke emotion, which often leads to viewers taking action. Project Renewal, an organization whose mission is to end the cycle of homelessness by empowering individuals and families to renew their lives with health, homes, and jobs, created a powerful video telling Lisa's personal story of renewing hope.

The video allows viewers to connect emotionally with Lisa's courageous journey and understand the real-world impact of the organization's work. It's a perfect example of how visual storytelling can bring your mission to life in a way that words alone often can't.

Example: Mercy Ships Canada Web Story

Sharing personal stories is not easy, especially for those involved, but Mercy Ships Canada does a wonderful job outlining the lives of those they serve. They have a section on their website dedicated to personal, heart-grabbing, real-life stories. One example is the story of Mercy, a woman from Guinea who needed critical surgery for a tumor growing on her face.

By sharing Mercy's story, including her struggles, the surgery process, and her recovery, Mercy Ships Canada creates a powerful narrative that demonstrates the tangible impact of their work while honoring the experiences of those they serve.

Storytelling Across Different Nonprofit Sectors

While the core principles of storytelling remain consistent, the approach can vary across different types of nonprofits:

- **Environmental Organizations:** Focus on before-and-after narratives that showcase the tangible impact of conservation efforts. Use vivid imagery and data visualization to illustrate changes over time.
- **Example:** The Nature Conservancy often uses time-lapse photography to show the restoration of ecosystems, combining visual storytelling with hard data.

- **Healthcare Nonprofits:** Prioritize patient stories that highlight both the challenges of illness and the hope provided by medical interventions. Ensure you have proper consent and maintain patient privacy.
- **Example:** St. Jude Children's Research Hospital shares stories of young patients and their families, focusing on their journeys and the impact of donations on their treatment.
- **Education Nonprofits:** Highlight individual student success stories and the long-term impact of educational programs. Use metrics like graduation rates or career achievements to support these narratives.
- **Example:** Teach for America features stories of both teachers and students, showing the mutual growth and impact of their educational programs.
- **Human Rights Organizations:** Balance the need to showcase urgent issues with stories of resilience and positive change. Use a mix of personal testimonies and broader contextual narratives.
- **Example:** Amnesty International often combines individual stories of human rights defenders with broader campaigns about systemic issues.

Overcoming Common Storytelling Challenges

Now, I know what you're thinking. "Tammy, this all sounds great in theory, but what about the real-world challenges we face?" Don't worry, I've got you covered. Let's tackle some common storytelling obstacles and how to overcome them:

- **Lack of Compelling Narratives**
  - **Challenge:** You're struggling to find personal stories that resonate with your audience. Maybe you work in a field where privacy concerns make it difficult to share individual stories, or perhaps you're having trouble capturing the experiences of those who have benefited from your programs.
  - **Solution:** Get creative with your storytelling sources. Consider:
    - **Collaborative Storytelling:** Work with individuals who have benefited from your programs to co-create stories they're proud to share.

- **Composite Stories:** Create narratives that combine elements from multiple real experiences while protecting individual privacy.
- **Staff and Volunteer Stories:** Share the perspectives of those on the front lines of your work.

- **Limited Resources for Storytelling**
  - **Challenge:** You're a small nonprofit with limited staff and financial resources. Professional videography or design services for storytelling seem out of reach.
  - **Solution:** Embrace the power of user-generated content and social media:
    - Encourage supporters and volunteers to share their experiences through photos, videos, or written posts.
    - Use free or low-cost tools like Canva for creating visually appealing graphics.
    - Leverage smartphone cameras and free editing apps to create simple but effective videos.

- **Complex and Technical Subject Matter**
  - **Challenge:** Your nonprofit focuses on complex issues or technical subjects that are difficult to translate into engaging stories for the general public.
  - **Solution:** Use storytelling techniques to simplify complex concepts:
    - Use analogies and metaphors to explain difficult concepts in relatable terms.
    - Create narrative arcs that follow the journey of a specific project, highlighting key discoveries and challenges.
    - Collaborate with science communicators or journalists to help bridge the gap between technical jargon and engaging storytelling.

- **Overcoming Donor Fatigue**
  - **Challenge:** You've been addressing a long-standing social issue, and you're noticing a decline in donor engagement over time. Donors seem desensitized to your usual storytelling approaches.

- **Solution:** Find fresh angles and perspectives to rekindle donor interest:
    - Highlight innovative approaches or partnerships your organization is exploring.
    - Share stories of unexpected positive ripple effects in your community from your collaborative work.
    - Incorporate interactive elements or gamification into your storytelling to create a more engaging experience.
- **Balancing Impact and Ethics**
    - **Challenge:** You want to create impactful stories, but you're concerned about exploiting the individuals or communities you serve for the sake of fundraising.
    - **Solution:** Develop clear ethical guidelines for storytelling within your organization:
        - Obtain informed consent from individuals featured in stories.
        - Prioritize the dignity and agency of those you serve in your storytelling efforts.
        - Focus on strength-based stories of empowerment and resilience rather than victimhood.

Enhancing Cultural Sensitivity in Storytelling

Cultural sensitivity is crucial when crafting narratives about diverse communities. Here are some practical tips to ensure your stories are respectful and inclusive:

- **Research Thoroughly:** Before telling a story about a specific culture or community, invest time in understanding their customs, values, and sensitivities. Consult with cultural experts or community leaders from that community for guidance.
- **Use Appropriate Language:** Be mindful of the terms and phrases you use. What might seem harmless in one culture could be offensive in another. For example, avoid using terms like "tribe" when referring to Indigenous communities unless specifically requested by the community.
- **Avoid Stereotypes:** Challenge preconceptions rather than reinforcing them. For instance, when telling stories about communities in

developing countries, focus on their resilience and innovation rather than portraying them as victims.

- **Represent Diversity Within Cultures:** Remember that cultures are not monolithic. Even within a single community, there can be a wide range of experiences and perspectives. Strive to showcase this diversity in your storytelling.
- **Empower Local Voices:** Whenever possible, let people from the communities you serve tell their own stories. This not only ensures authenticity but also respects their agency.

Example: The International Rescue Committee often features stories told by refugees themselves, allowing them to share their experiences in their own words. This approach ensures cultural authenticity and gives voice to those directly affected by the issues.

Measuring the Effectiveness of Your Storytelling

Now, I know you're probably wondering, "How do I know if my storytelling efforts are actually working?" Great question! Let's dive into some effective ways to measure the impact of your narratives and track the success of your storytelling efforts.

- **Engagement Metrics:** Use tools like Google Analytics or social media insights to measure how long people spend interacting with your stories online. Track metrics such as page views, time spent on page, social media shares, and comments. These can indicate how compelling your audience finds your stories.
- **Conversion Rate:** Monitor changes in donation patterns and track how many people take a desired action (e.g., donating, volunteering) after engaging with a story. Tools like UTM (urchin tracking module) parameters can help attribute these actions to specific stories. Look at both the number of donations and the average donation amount.
- **Share of Voice:** Employ media monitoring tools like Meltwater or Brandwatch to measure how much your organization's stories are being discussed compared to similar organizations or topics. This can

help you gauge your storytelling's impact on brand awareness and public perception.

- **Sentiment Analysis:** Use AI-powered tools like Hootsuite Insights or Sprout Social to analyze the emotional response to your stories in comments and social media mentions. This can provide valuable insights into how your stories resonate with your audience.

- **Long-term Relationship Metrics:** Track metrics related to donor retention and long-term engagement. Use your CRM (customer relationship management system) to monitor donor lifetime value, comparing those who engage with your stories to those who don't. Effective storytelling should not only drive immediate donations, volunteer inquiries, and advocacy sign-ups but also foster lasting relationships with supporters.

- **Surveys and Feedback:** Regularly survey your donors, volunteers, community partners, and program participants to gather qualitative feedback on your storytelling efforts. Ask questions about which stories resonated most and why.

- **A/B Testing:** Test different storytelling approaches against each other to see which generates better results. This could involve testing different narrative structures, media formats, or calls to action.

- **Mission Impact:** Ultimately, the goal of your storytelling is to further your mission. Develop metrics that tie your storytelling efforts to real-world impact in the communities you serve.

Remember, the most important metrics will depend on your specific goals and the nature of your organization. Regularly review and adjust your measurement strategies to ensure they're providing valuable insights that can inform your storytelling approach. By employing a combination of these metrics and tools, you'll gain a comprehensive understanding of your storytelling effectiveness and be better equipped to refine your strategies for maximum impact.

Engaging Volunteers and Staff in Storytelling

Involving your volunteers and staff in the storytelling process can provide authentic perspectives and expand your storytelling capabilities:

- **Create a Story Bank:** Develop a system where donors, volunteers, community members, and staff can easily submit their experiences and observations. This could be a simple online form or a dedicated email address.
- **Provide Training:** Offer workshops on basic storytelling techniques, photography, and video creation, as well as your consent policies and practices. This empowers your team to capture and share stories effectively and ethically.
- **Implement a "Story of the Month" Program:** Regularly feature stories from different volunteers and staff members across your communication channels. This not only provides fresh content but also recognizes their contributions.
- **Use Peer Interviews:** Encourage volunteers and advocates to interview each other about their experiences. This can lead to more relaxed and authentic storytelling.
- **Create Collaborative Content:** Involve multiple team members in creating larger storytelling projects, like an annual impact report or a video series.
- **Leverage Social Media Takeovers:** Allow skilled and trusted volunteers, advocates, or staff to "take over" your social media accounts for a day, sharing their perspectives and experiences in real time.

Example: The Red Cross often features stories from their volunteers on the ground during disaster relief efforts, providing immediate, authentic accounts of their work.

By implementing these strategies, you can create a more inclusive, effective, and diverse storytelling approach that resonates across various nonprofit sectors and engages your entire team in the process.

The Future of Nonprofit Storytelling: Embracing Technology

As we look to the future, it's clear that technology will play an increasingly important role in nonprofit storytelling. Here are some trends and strategies to consider:

- **AI and Automation:** Artificial intelligence tools are helping teams personalize donor outreach, optimize messaging, and free up time for high-impact work. While these tools should be used responsibly and in conjunction with human oversight, they can significantly enhance your storytelling capabilities.

For example, AI can help analyze large amounts of data to identify trends and insights that can inform your storytelling strategy. It can also assist in personalizing stories for different donor segments, ensuring that each narrative resonates with its intended audience.

- **Integrated Data Systems:** Centralized and integrated data systems will give nonprofits an advantage in personalizing outreach, tracking donor behavior more effectively, and growing engagement. By leveraging data, you can create more targeted and impactful stories that resonate with specific donor segments.

These systems can help you understand which types of stories resonate most with different donor groups, allowing you to tailor your narratives for maximum impact. They can also help you track the journey of individual donors, allowing you to craft stories that speak to their specific interests and giving history.

- **Video Storytelling:** Video has already transformed donor engagement, and its role will only grow in the years ahead. Younger donors, in particular, expect video and multimedia content that makes them feel something. Invest in video content that showcases beneficiary journeys, illustrates the impact of donations, or provides behind-the-scenes glimpses of your work.

Consider exploring new video formats like vertical videos for social media platforms, live streaming for real-time engagement, or even 360-degree videos for immersive experiences.

- **Virtual and Augmented Reality (VR/AR):** While still emerging technologies in the nonprofit sector, virtual and augmented reality offer exciting possibilities for immersive storytelling. These technologies could allow donors to "experience" the impact of their contributions firsthand, creating powerful emotional connections to your cause.

For example, a conservation nonprofit could use VR to transport donors to a rainforest they're working to protect, or an education-focused organization could use AR to show how a donation could transform a classroom.

- **Interactive Storytelling:** Interactive storytelling techniques, where the audience can participate in or influence the narrative, are becoming increasingly popular. This could involve choose-your-own-adventure style stories on your website, interactive infographics, or even simple polls and quizzes that engage donors while telling your organization's story.

The Human Moment in Storytelling

As we embrace these technological advancements, it's crucial to remember that at the heart of effective storytelling lies in what Dr. Edward M. Hallowell calls the "human moment." This is an authentic psychological encounter that can only happen when two people share the same physical space, demanding focused emotional and intellectual involvement.

While digital tools can enhance our storytelling capabilities, they should never replace the power of face-to-face interactions and genuine human connections. The most impactful stories are those that create a bridge between the donor, the nonprofit, and the community being served, fostering a sense of shared purpose and mutual understanding.

As fundraisers and nonprofit leaders, our challenge is to harness the power of both technology and human connection in our storytelling efforts. By doing so, we can create narratives that not only inspire donations, volunteerism, and advocacy but also build lasting relationships and drive meaningful change in our communities.

Key Takeaways and Action Steps

- **Identify Your Core Message:** Clearly define the problem your organization is solving and your unique approach. Use this as the foundation for all your storytelling efforts.

- **Develop a Story Bank:** Create a collection of stories from beneficiaries, donors, community members, staff, and volunteers. Regularly update this bank to ensure you always have fresh, compelling narratives to share.
- **Embrace Multimedia:** Invest in various forms of storytelling, including written content, photos, videos, and potentially even virtual or augmented reality experiences.
- **Personalize Your Stories:** Use data and technology to tailor your stories to different donor segments, ensuring maximum relevance and impact.
- **Prioritize Ethical Storytelling:** Develop clear guidelines for ethical storytelling within your organization, ensuring that you respect the dignity and privacy of those featured in your stories.
- **Leverage Technology:** Explore how AI, automation, and integrated data systems can enhance your storytelling capabilities while freeing up time for high-impact work.
- **Foster Human Connections:** While embracing technology, don't forget the power of face-to-face interactions and authentic human moments in your storytelling efforts.
- **Measure and Adapt:** Regularly assess the impact of your storytelling efforts. Use analytics to understand which stories resonate most with your audience and adapt your approach accordingly.
- **Train Your Team:** Invest in storytelling training for your staff and volunteers. The more people in your organization who can effectively tell your story, the greater your impact will be.
- **Create Opportunities for Donor Involvement:** Find ways to involve donors in your storytelling process, whether through user-generated content, donor spotlight stories, or interactive experiences.

Practical Exercise: Crafting Your Narrative

To put what you've learned into practice, try this exercise:

- Identify a recent success story or impactful moment from your organization's work.
- Write a brief (300–500 words) narrative about this moment, incorporating the storytelling principles we've discussed.

- Create two versions of this story—one for a traditional written format and one adapted for social media (consider how you might break it into shorter posts or incorporate visual elements).
- Share these stories with a small group (colleagues, board members, trusted donors, community volunteers, or staff) and gather feedback.
- Based on the feedback, refine your stories and consider how you might expand them into a larger campaign.

The Ongoing Journey of Storytelling Excellence

Storytelling is a skill that improves with practice. The more you engage in crafting and sharing narratives related to your organization's work, the more effective you'll become at creating stories that resonate and inspire action. Don't fall into the trap of telling just *your* favorite story. Tell stories that inspire the outcome you desire from the story listener or reader- be a strategic storyteller.

By implementing these strategies and continuously refining your approach, you can harness the power of storytelling to create a truly human-centered approach to fundraising. Remember, every story you tell is an opportunity to connect, inspire, and drive positive change. Make each one count.

As we move forward into the next chapter, we'll explore how to cultivate major gifts by advancing donors. The storytelling techniques we've discussed here will play a crucial role in this process, helping you create meaningful connections with potential major donors (and anyone else) and illustrate the impact of their contributions. So, keep these storytelling principles in mind as we delve into the art of donor advancement in the chapters to come.

Navigating Power Dynamics in Human-Centered Fundraising

"We can disagree and still love each other, unless your disagreement is rooted in my oppression and denial of my humanity and right to exist."

—James Baldwin, Author & LGBTQ+ Activist

As I reflect on my journey in the nonprofit sector, I am reminded of the intricate web of power dynamics that underpin every interaction between fundraisers, nonprofit leadership, donors, board members, funders, and those we serve through our programs and services. Power itself isn't good or bad. We all have power. But when power is unbalanced, weaponized, and left unchecked, it can diminish people, erode trust, destroy an organization's culture, and bring our missions to a screeching halt.

Envision power dynamics as a puzzle where each piece represents a stakeholder. When all the pieces fit together harmoniously, the picture is complete, and the nonprofit thrives. However, if some pieces are missing or don't fit well, the puzzle remains incomplete, reflecting the challenges of unaddressed power imbalances. This chapter will delve into the challenges posed by these dynamics and provide practical strategies for navigating them, all while maintaining a human-centered approach to fundraising.

Introduction to Power Dynamics

Imagine a grand symphony where each player has a unique role, but some instruments are louder than others. In the nonprofit world, this symphony is played out in the relationships between stakeholders. Funders, donors, and board members often hold significant influence, while fundraisers, volunteers, and community members may feel their voices are muted. This imbalance can lead to missed opportunities, strained relationships, and ultimately less effective fundraising.

Power dynamics are not inherently bad; they are a natural part of any social interaction. However, when these dynamics are not acknowledged or managed, they can hinder collaboration and innovation. For instance, a funder might dictate how funds are used, limiting a nonprofit's ability to respond to community needs effectively. Similarly, a board member's influence can overshadow the expertise of nonprofit staff, leading to decisions that might not align with the organization's mission.

Power Dynamics in Human-Centered Fundraising

Understanding and managing power dynamics is crucial in human-centered fundraising. After all, one of the top challenges with donor-centered fundraising has been our hesitancy to speak truth to power when our donors *(especially major donors and board members)* cross the line. When they hold a myth, misconception, or stereotype about our work or those we serve as truth, and we fundraisers don't speak up. We passively smile and fawn for fear of losing the donor and their contributions or worse, we fear retaliation. Acquiescing to donor power was never the intent of donor-centered fundraising.

Fundraisers also have power, and it is our responsibility to acknowledge the inherent power imbalances between organizations and donors, and to foster relationships built on transparency, mutual respect, and genuine engagement. Effective fundraising involves not just asking for funds but also building genuine partnerships that acknowledge and navigate these power structures thoughtfully.

Culturally, it's only natural to acquiesce in many of these situations. Generational factors such as age, gender, race, wealth, and social status all play a role. Many of us were raised hearing messages like "respect your elders," "it's rude to talk about money," and "don't talk back." Many of us were raised in homes where the father figure was the dominant presence. It's no wonder we fear pushing back or respectfully correcting misconceptions, stereotypes, and untruths of those we consciously or subconsciously deem more powerful than us. And still, we must push back, nonetheless. A few example sentence stems that have helped me as a fundraiser navigating power dynamics include:

- "Interesting, say more about that *(misconception, stereotype, or myth)*"
- "Can you give me an example?"
- "Help me understand… ."
- "A few others have shared that perspective with me. Here's what I've learned since working here: [insert corrected perception]"
- "I'm interested in what you're saying. Can you tell me more about why you think that?"

I've learned to suspend my personal values and judgment until I understand their point of view and then respectfully redirect them to the beliefs and values of the mission. Curiosity and empathy are key as you search for common ground. If in the end, they don't share any of your organization's beliefs and values—or are vehemently opposed to them—they aren't your people, no matter their wealth or influence. Let me say that again for the people in the back: if they don't share any of your organization's beliefs and values, they aren't your people, no matter their wealth or influence. "Bless and release," as a wise mentor used to say.

Let me tell you a story from my days on the frontline of fundraising related to power dynamics. I had just presented a stewardship report chock-full of inspiring stories and impressive outcomes to a large group of donors at their annual membership reception. Afterward, a long-time major donor approached me with a question. *"Which ones are the smart ones?"* If you could hear my thoughts in that moment, you'd hear the cool-down count: 5, 4, 3, 2, 1. I silently said to myself, don't make assumptions, Tammy. So, I asked her to say more. *"You know, the ones who live off the system versus trying to pull themselves up by the bootstraps?"* Now you have to know I love the families in our programs. They inspire me with their tenacity and strength—overcoming challenges they had no hand in creating. I replied, *"I suppose maybe 2% of them may have learned to live off the system as a survival strategy as a result of decades of institutional racism and generational poverty. Maybe 2% of them have the necessary resources and support systems to pull themselves up by the bootstraps. I get up every morning for the remaining 96% of children and families who are working hard to make a better life for themselves. And I'm sure that's why you're such a generous supporter too."* If I couldn't hold the space of dignity and respect for the children and families my organization served, I didn't deserve the honor of representing them and their stories as a fundraiser.

Current Trends and Best Practices

In recent years, there has been a growing emphasis on responsible and beneficial integration of AI in fundraising to help personalize donor interactions and streamline processes. However, it's crucial to ensure that AI tools do not exacerbate existing power imbalances by marginalizing certain voices or perspectives and perpetuating bias.

Another trend is the rise of subscription giving, which offers nonprofits a predictable revenue stream and fosters donor loyalty. This model can be particularly effective when combined with human-centered fundraising strategies, as it encourages ongoing engagement and support.

Challenges in Power Dynamics

- **Inequitable Influence:** One of the most significant challenges we face is the uneven distribution of power. Funders and board members often have more sway over decision-making processes than community members or nonprofit staff. This can result in decisions that prioritize the interests and perceived priorities of those in power over the needs of the community being served.

- **Fear of Retaliation:** Another challenge is the fear of speaking up against those with more power. Nonprofit staff might hesitate to provide honest feedback to funders or board members, fearing repercussions that could impact funding or job security.
- **Lack of Representation:** Beneficiaries or community members are often excluded from decision-making tables, further marginalizing their voices and perspectives.

Solutions and Strategies

To navigate these challenges effectively, we need a toolkit of strategies that promote equity, transparency, and collaboration.

- **Inclusive Decision-Making:** Involve community members and beneficiaries in decision-making processes. This can be achieved by creating advisory boards or community councils that have a formal role in guiding organizational decisions.
- **Transparent Communication:** Foster open and honest communication channels. Regular feedback sessions and transparent reporting can help build trust between stakeholders and ensure that everyone's voice is heard.
- **Empowerment Through Education:** Educate all stakeholders about the importance of equitable power dynamics. This includes training on cultural competence, equity, and inclusion to address implicit biases and privilege.
- **Adapting Tools for Different Sectors:** The strategies mentioned above can be adapted across various nonprofit sectors. For example, in healthcare nonprofits, community advisory boards can ensure that services are tailored to meet local health needs. In education nonprofits, involving students and parents in decision-making can lead to more effective programs.

Power Dynamics Across Nonprofit Sectors

Power dynamics play out differently across various nonprofit sectors. Let's explore a few examples:

1. **Healthcare Nonprofits:** In healthcare, power dynamics often revolve around the relationship between medical professionals and patients. For example, the Camden Coalition uses the COACH framework to empower care teams to form authentic healing relationships, shifting power dynamics by involving patients more deeply in their care plans. This approach not only improves patient outcomes but also fosters a sense of community and shared responsibility.

2. **Education Nonprofits:** In education, power dynamics can be influenced by the hierarchical structure of schools. Organizations like Haiti Partners Inc. have found success by listening to and involving students and community members in decision-making processes, which helps build trust and stronger partnerships.

3. **Environmental Nonprofits:** Environmental organizations often navigate complex local and global power dynamics. For instance, WaterNet, a water-focused nonprofit, must balance local community needs with global sustainability goals, using networked publics to engage diverse stakeholders effectively.

Addressing Resistance from Stakeholders

Overcoming resistance from stakeholders, such as board members or funders, requires a thoughtful approach:

- **Conduct Stakeholder Analysis:** Identify key stakeholders and assess their influence, interest, and potential resistance level. This helps tailor strategies to address their concerns proactively.
- **Open Communication Channels:** Establish transparent communication to address concerns and involve stakeholders in decision-making processes. This fosters a sense of ownership and reduces resistance.

- **Change Champions:** Identify and enlist change champions within the organization who can advocate for new practices and help disseminate positive messaging.
- **Training and Development:** Provide training to equip stakeholders with the skills needed for change, enhancing their capabilities and reducing apprehension.

The Role of Technology in Power Dynamics

Technology can both exacerbate and mitigate power imbalances:

- **Amplifying Marginalized Voices:** Digital platforms can amplify marginalized and historically excluded voices by providing accessible channels for feedback and engagement. For example, social media can be used to share stories and perspectives from community members, ensuring their voices are heard in decision-making processes if they have public or private access to digital tools such as computers and/or smartphones.
- **Equitable Access to Information:** Technology can help ensure equitable access to information by making data and resources available to all stakeholders. This can help level the playing field and reduce information disparities that contribute to power imbalances. But it's important to confirm your constituents have public or private access to technology and are functional users.
- **Data-Driven Decision Making:** Technology can facilitate data-driven decision-making, allowing nonprofits to track and analyze donor behavior, which can inform more inclusive fundraising strategies.

During my work with The Children's Center in Detroit, we faced significant fundraising challenges due to outdated systems and a lack of community engagement. By embracing a human-centered approach, we engaged the community in our decision-making processes through a Consumer Council, board, and committee service, Town Halls, and hosted conversations and panels. This led to a tripling of philanthropy within three years and a doubling again six years later. The key was not just in the numbers but in the relationships we built and the trust we earned from our community, volunteer, and donor base.

Concrete Metrics for Success

To measure the success of strategies aimed at addressing power dynamics, consider the following metrics:

- **Inclusive Decision-Making Participation:** Track the number of community members involved in decision-making processes and their reported satisfaction with these processes.
- **Donor Retention Rates:** Measure how inclusive practices impact donor retention, as nonprofits that track unconventional KPIs like community engagement often see increased donor loyalty.
- **Community Engagement Levels:** Monitor the level of community engagement and feedback, which can indicate the effectiveness of inclusive strategies.

Inclusive Decision-Making Processes

Creating inclusive decision-making processes involves several practical steps:

- **Set Up Advisory Councils:** Establish community advisory councils with clear charters, term limits, and recruitment procedures to ensure diverse representation.
- **Clarify Decision-Making Processes:** Make clear who will decide and who will provide input, setting transparent timelines for decision-making.
- **Build Input Mechanisms:** Use surveys, interviews, or focus groups to gather input from stakeholders, ensuring representation and inclusivity.
- **Collaboratively Define Decision Factors:** Involve stakeholders in defining the factors that will guide decision-making, ensuring their concerns are reflected.

Empowerment Through Education

Empowering stakeholders through education involves:

- **Training Programs:** Offer ongoing workshops on power dynamics, equity, and inclusion to help stakeholders, including staff, board, and committees, understand and address power imbalances.
- **Case Studies:** Use real-world examples to illustrate the impact of inclusive practices and the challenges of navigating power dynamics.
- **Feedback Loops:** Establish continuous feedback loops to capture ongoing concerns and adjust strategies accordingly.

Adapting Strategies Across Sectors

Adapting strategies to different sectors requires understanding the unique power dynamics at play:

- **Healthcare:** Involve patients in care planning and decision-making processes to enhance patient-centered care.
- **Education:** Engage students and community members in educational planning to foster more inclusive learning environments.
- **Environmental:** Balance local community needs with global sustainability goals through networked publics and inclusive stakeholder engagement.

Key Takeaways and Action Steps

Navigating power dynamics in fundraising requires empathy, understanding, courage, and a commitment to equity. Here are the key takeaways and action steps you can implement immediately:

- **Acknowledge Power Imbalances:** Recognize the power dynamics at play in your organization and work to address them.
- **Foster Inclusive Decision-Making:** Involve community members and beneficiaries in decision-making processes.
- **Promote Transparent Communication:** Establish open and honest communication channels.

- **Empower Through Education:** Provide training on equity and inclusion to address implicit biases. Consider making it mandatory for constituent groups who traditional hold power such as board and committee members, and executive leadership.
- **Adapt Strategies Across Sectors:** Tailor your approach to fit the unique needs of your nonprofit sector.
- **Leverage Technology:** Use digital platforms to amplify marginalized voices and ensure equitable access to information.

By embracing these strategies, you can create a more equitable and effective fundraising environment that truly serves your community. Remember, the journey to a human-centered approach is ongoing, and it requires continuous learning and adaptation. Let's work together to build a future where every nonprofit thrives, and every community has the support it needs to flourish.

As we navigate the complex landscape of power dynamics, it becomes clear that successful fundraising is not just about securing funds; it's about building relationships and fostering a sense of community. In the next chapter, we will explore how human-centered fundraising can be a powerful tool in bridging gaps between donors, community members, and nonprofit leaders. By crafting narratives that resonate with all stakeholders, we can create a shared vision that drives collective action and supports our mission.

9 | The Hero's Journey: Implementing the Human-Centered Model

"Heroes are ordinary people who make themselves extraordinary."
—Gerard Way, American Singer, Songwriter,
Comic Book Writer, and Producer

As you embark on your journey to implement a human-centered fundraising approach, remember that you are not alone. You are a hero, among a league of heroes. Yes, donors are heroes. Volunteers are heroes. Community Advocates are Heroes. Staff are Heroes. The people who participate in your programs, patients, students, families, homebound friends and neighbors, gifted artists, and rising leaders are *all* heroes. Each with unique gifts, expertise, and influence to share. Each with hopes and dreams for themselves, and the causes for which they care deeply. No hero is elevated above another; rather, each is recognized as a crucial partner in our collective progress.

Like the heroes of ancient myths, you are answering a call to adventure—one that will transform not only your organization and community, but the entire landscape of philanthropy. This chapter will serve as your guide, providing you with a roadmap to navigate opportunities that lie ahead.

The Call to Adventure: Assessing Your Current Practices

Every hero's journey begins with a call to adventure, and yours starts with a thorough assessment of your current fundraising and community engagement practices. This crucial first step will help you identify areas of strength as well as areas for improvement and establish a baseline for measuring your progress.

Conducting a Fundraising Audit

Begin by conducting a comprehensive audit of your existing fundraising strategies, tools, and outcomes. This process should involve:

- Analyzing your donor database and established key metrics.
- Reviewing your communication strategies and channels. Are you reaching your intended constituents effectively? How do you measure effectiveness?
- Evaluating your annual fund, major gifts, and legacy giving programs. What's working and could possibly be scaled? What's not working, and could be reimagined to be more effective or sunset entirely to free up time and resources for strategies with higher return on investment? What's missing because you haven't had sufficient time, resources, or expertise?
- Assessing your team's skills, capacity, gaps, and well-being

The Fundraising Effectiveness Project (FEP) report, underwritten by the Association of Fundraising Professionals (AFP) Foundation for Philanthropy, reveals that only 19% of first-year donors gave again in 2024, and fewer than 50% of second-year donors continued, leading to a constant, costly cycle of donor replacement. This transactional approach not only drains resources but also erodes trust and staff morale. As you conduct your audit, specifically calculate your donor retention rates and compare them to sector benchmarks. Make retention a central metric in your board and staff discussions, not just cash raised. This shift in focus is foundational to a relational, human-centered approach.

As you conduct this audit, ask yourself: How well do our current practices align with human-centered principles? Are we truly putting people—donors, volunteers, community ambassadors, beneficiaries, and staff—at the heart of our fundraising and community engagement efforts? Are we building genuine relationships with them? Do they feel seen, heard, and understood? Are we effectively engaging colleagues across the entire organization to collaborate with us in constituent engagement where possible and appropriate?

Gathering Stakeholder Feedback

Your journey toward human-centered fundraising cannot be a solitary one. Engage your stakeholders—including staff, board members, volunteers, donors, and community members—in the assessment process. Their perspectives will provide valuable insights and help build buy-in for the changes to come.

Consider using surveys, focus groups, town halls, and one-on-one interviews to gather feedback. Ask questions such as:

- How well do you feel our current fundraising and community engagement approach aligns with our mission?
- In what ways do you feel valued and engaged by our organization?
- What suggestions do you have for improving our community engagement practices and fundraising approaches?
- How could we improve our community engagement and fundraising strategies?

Imagine if your development team members committed to calling 10 everyday donors or volunteers each month and asking them how they are, why they give, and how they feel about their relationship with your organization. What if your Executive Director and Board Members did the same?

This simple relational practice yields powerful insights and helps donors feel genuinely valued. Universities routinely recruit students to join their call center teams, thanking donors for the specific support they provide—scholarships, endowed professorships, athletics, and so on. How many volunteers receive a similar phone call? How many community advocates? What about consumer council members or program committee participants? Do they receive those phone calls? It's far less common, making all the more meaningful when it does happen.

By authentically engaging and expressing gratitude to your stakeholders from the outset, you're not only gathering crucial information but also laying the groundwork for a more collaborative, human-centered approach.

Crossing the Threshold: Developing Your Human-Centered Strategy

With a clear understanding of your current practices and stakeholder perspectives, you're ready to cross the threshold into the special world of human-centered fundraising. This next phase of your journey involves developing a strategy that puts people at the heart of your fundraising efforts. But first, a reminder that Rome wasn't built in a day. Too often, we build our strategies around a fiscal year and become disillusioned if transformation doesn't occur in twelve fleeting months. Yes, some strategies will yield positive results in a year or less. Some strategies will require investment that may not yield a return for two years or more. Your greatest success will be achieved when your strategy strikes a balance between short and long-term yields, encompassing the three pillars of annual fund, major gifts, and planned giving—centered on a people-first, human-centered approach.

Defining Your Human-Centered Vision

Begin by articulating a clear vision for what human-centered fundraising entails within your organization. This vision should reflect both your mission and the feedback you've gathered from stakeholders. It might include elements such as:

- Building authentic, long-term relationships with donors and community members

- Engaging community members as genuine partners in the work
- Ensuring transparency and accountability in all communication and fundraising activities
- Prioritizing the dignity and agency of those you serve
- Developing programs for, with, and by our community

Your vision will serve as a north star, guiding your decisions and actions as you implement your new approach.

Setting Human-Centered Goals

With your vision in place, it's time to set specific, measurable goals that will help you realize it. These goals should go beyond traditional fundraising metrics to encompass the broader impact of your human-centered approach. Consider goals such as:

- Increasing donor retention rates by W%
- Engaging X% more community members in program design and evaluation
- Reducing staff burnout and turnover by Y%
- Improving beneficiary satisfaction scores by Z points

Include donor retention rates as a core organizational metric. Make it a regular part of board agendas and report on it alongside revenue. Peter Drucker, often referred to as the Father of Modern Management, emphasizes that what gets measured gets managed-so make retention and donor satisfaction central to your success metrics.

Remember, the key to human-centered fundraising is balancing the needs and perspectives of all stakeholders—donors, community members, staff, and beneficiaries alike.

Mapping Your Donor and Community Journeys

A crucial step in developing your human-centered strategy is mapping out the journeys of your donors and community members. This process involves identifying all the touchpoints where these stakeholders interact with your organization and considering how to make each interaction more meaningful and impactful. Segmenting your donors and mapping unique donor journeys for first-time donors, monthly giving members, mid-level givers, leadership givers, major donors, and legacy donors will yield the best results. They are each special and deserve personalized engagement, whether it be digital, in-person, or some combination of outreach channels.

For donors and volunteers, this might include:

- Initial awareness of your organization
- First donation or volunteer experience
- Thank you, and impact reporting
- Ongoing engagement and stewardship
- Repeat volunteerism, donations, or increased giving

For community members, the journey might look like:

- Identifying community needs
- Co-creating program solutions
- Participating in program implementation
- Providing feedback and evaluation
- Becoming advocates, volunteers, or donors themselves

We suggest identifying your top donor (or constituent) personas and mapping an ideal journey for each of them, focusing on how each touchpoint makes them feel. Consider questions like: Are we telling compelling stories? Are we asking for input? Are we providing opportunities for deeper involvement in the areas of our work that they're most passionate about? Utilize direct feedback to refine these touchpoints, ensuring each step is meaningful and relational.

By mapping these journeys, you can identify opportunities to infuse human-centered principles at every stage, creating a more holistic and engaging experience for all stakeholders. Sounds laborious, right? That's the beauty of AI-powered automated workflows for some segments of your constituents. Not everyone wants a personal relationship with you, but they do want a relationship with your organization through quality communication and engagement. Plan those high-quality touchpoints into your automated workflows. Also plan them into your engagement strategies for high-touch donors assigned to gift officer portfolios. The truth is that every donor and engaged constituent should have a combination of digital and personal touchpoints throughout the year, the ratio of digital versus personal touchpoints is dependent on them and their needs.

Tests and Allies: Building Your Human-Centered Infrastructure

As you venture deeper into your hero's journey, you'll encounter tests and challenges. But you'll also find allies and tools to help you overcome these obstacles. This phase of your journey involves building the infrastructure and culture needed to support your human-centered approach.

Investing in Technology

The right technology can be a powerful ally in your quest for human-centered fundraising. Look for tools that can help you:

- Centralize and analyze donor data
- Utilize predictive analytics to reveal patterns and insights
- Personalize communications at scale
- Facilitate community engagement and feedback
- Track and report on impact metrics

Artificial Intelligence (AI) can segment donor lists, predict giving patterns, and automate personalized communications, making it possible to treat every donor as an individual, not just major donors. For example, MAZON: A Jewish Response to Hunger, an organization that has battled hunger for 40 years, increased appeal revenue by 23% while sending 10% fewer letters by using AI to target messages more effectively. AI-driven tools can also automate thank-you letters, optimize messaging timing, and identify donors at risk of lapsing, freeing up staff for high-touch engagement.

Remember, technology should enhance, not replace, human connections. Choose tools that free up your team's time for meaningful interactions with donors and community members.

Thinking you don't have the budget to invest in technology? Consider that a 10% increase in donor retention can more than double the lifetime value of your donor file, according to Dr. Adrian Sargeant, Co-Founder of the Institute for Sustainable Philanthropy. Imagine that a single major gift could likely cover the costs of these tools! Run the return on investment numbers and make a case for investing in fundraising infrastructure.

Developing Your Team's Skills

Your staff are your most important allies on this journey. Invest in their development by providing training in areas such as:

- Relationship-building and donor stewardship
- Community engagement and facilitation
- Storytelling and impact communication
- Data analysis and interpretation

Adopt relational fundraising practices such as:

- Thanking donors at scale (using video tools or board member thank-you calls)
- Replacing some solicitations with stories to foster emotional connection
- Creating giving circles or peer communities for deeper engagement
- Calling a set of donors monthly to ask about their motivations and experiences

These practices are scalable, can be automated, are low-cost, and can be piloted immediately to foster a culture of innovation and learning.

Consider partnering with organizations like the Association of Fundraising Professionals (AFP) or the Nonprofit Technology Network (NTEN), Fundraising. AI, and the Modern Institute for Charitable Giving for professional development opportunities.

Fostering a Culture of Empathy and Learning

Human-centered fundraising requires more than just new strategies and skills—it demands a shift in organizational culture. Foster a culture of empathy, curiosity, and continuous learning by:

- Encouraging staff to spend time in the programs, connecting with those you serve and deepening your understanding of their lived experience
- Creating opportunities for donors to engage directly with your work and beneficiaries as appropriate. Remember, no one wants to be on display. Perhaps they volunteer with the homework help program, or deliver meals to homebound neighbors
- Regularly sharing stories and feedback from all stakeholders across the organization
- Celebrating failures as learning opportunities and encouraging innovation

Leadership buy-in is critical. Boards should regularly discuss donor retention and satisfaction, not just revenue. Staff should be empowered to question longstanding transactional practices and propose relational alternatives, even if these seem less "efficient" in the short term.

Remember, culture change takes time and consistent effort. Lead by example and be patient as your team adapts to this new approach. Recognize incremental culture shifts.

The Supreme Ordeal: Overcoming Challenges

Every hero's journey involves a supreme ordeal—a challenge that tests their resolve and forces them to grow. In implementing human-centered fundraising, you're likely to face several common challenges. Here's how to overcome them:

Challenge 1: Resistance to Change

Some staff or board members may resist the shift to a human-centered approach, fearing it will disrupt established practices or relationships.

Solution: Address fears head-on by clearly communicating the benefits of the new approach. Share success stories from other organizations that have made similar transitions. Involve skeptics in the planning process, giving them ownership over certain aspects of the change.

Challenge 2: Resource Constraints

Implementing a human-centered approach may require initial investments in technology, training, or additional staff time.

Solution: Start small and scale up. Begin with pilot projects that demonstrate the impact of the new approach. Use these early wins to make the case for further investment. Look for ways to reallocate existing resources more efficiently.

Challenge 3: Balancing Diverse Stakeholder Needs

Human-centered fundraising involves striking a balance between the sometimes conflicting needs and perspectives of donors, community members, and beneficiaries. Expect to feel discomfort at times and to lean into courageous conversations.

Solution: Create opportunities for dialogue between different stakeholder groups. Use techniques like participatory budgeting or community advisory boards to involve multiple perspectives in decision-making. Be transparent about trade-offs and how decisions are made.

Challenge 4: Measuring New Types of Impact

Traditional fundraising metrics may not capture the full impact of a human-centered approach.

Solution: Develop a balanced scorecard that includes both financial and non-financial metrics. Consider measures such as donor satisfaction, community engagement levels, and staff retention alongside traditional fundraising key performance indicators (KPIs). Invest in systems to capture and analyze both qualitative and quantitative feedback.

The Road Back: Implementing and Iterating

As you overcome these challenges, you'll find yourself on the road back—implementing your human-centered approach and continuously refining it based on feedback and results.

Creating an Implementation Roadmap

Develop a phased implementation plan that outlines key milestones and responsibilities. This might include:

- Phase 1 (Months 1–3): Pilot new donor stewardship practices
- Phase 2 (Months 4–6): Implement community feedback mechanisms
- Phase 3 (Months 7–9): Roll out new impact reporting processes
- Phase 4 (Months 10–12): Launch a comprehensive staff training program

Be sure to build in regular checkpoints for reviewing progress and adjusting to meet the timeline and your available resources. While we outline four phases over twelve months above, do not expect to fully implement this human-centered approach in just one year. Remember Simon Sinek's quote from Chapter 2: "What good is an idea if it remains an idea? Try. Experiment. Iterate. Fail. Try again. Change the world."

Embracing Agile Principles

Adopt an agile mindset, treating your implementation as a series of experiments rather than a fixed plan. This approach involves:

- Breaking large initiatives into smaller, manageable sprints
- Regularly seeking feedback from stakeholders
- Being willing to pivot or adjust based on what you learn
- Celebrating small wins and learning from setbacks

Craft discrete relational fundraising experiments, such as piloting thank-you calls, story-based communications, or new donor stewardship practices. Use the feedback from these experiments to iterate, improve, and share the results with your team and stakeholders.

By embracing agility, you can respond quickly to challenges and opportunities as they arise, keeping your approach truly human-centered.

Embracing Flexibility and Learning from Feedback

As you progress through the hero's journey of implementing a human-centered fundraising approach, it's crucial to emphasize the importance of flexibility and learning from feedback. This mindset is not just a tool for overcoming challenges but a core principle that ensures your strategy remains vibrant and effective over time.

Why Flexibility Matters

In the dynamic world of nonprofit fundraising, circumstances can change rapidly. Donor preferences shift, community needs evolve, and technological advancements offer new opportunities. A flexible approach allows you to adapt quickly to these changes, ensuring that your fundraising efforts remain relevant and impactful. Whether it's adjusting your communication strategies or pivoting to new technologies, being open to change is essential for long-term success.

The Power of Feedback

Learning from feedback is the heartbeat of a human-centered approach. It involves not just listening to stakeholders but actively incorporating their insights into your strategy. This means regularly soliciting feedback from donors, community members, and your own team. By doing so, you create a culture of continuous improvement where every interaction is an opportunity to refine and enhance your fundraising practices.

Implementing Feedback Loops

To integrate feedback effectively, consider the following strategies:

- **Regular Surveys and Focus Groups:** Use these tools to gather structured feedback from stakeholders. This could include surveys to gauge donor satisfaction or focus groups to understand community perceptions of your organization.
- **Open Communication Channels:** Ensure that your organization has clear, accessible channels for stakeholders to provide feedback. This might include email, social media, or in-person meetings.

- **Data Analysis:** Use data analytics to track engagement metrics and identify areas where feedback suggests improvement is needed. This could involve analyzing website traffic, social media engagement, or email campaign metrics.
- **Agile Implementation:** Adopt an agile mindset by breaking down large initiatives into smaller, manageable projects. This allows you to test ideas, gather feedback, and adjust your approach quickly.

Embracing Failure as a Learning Opportunity

In the journey toward a human-centered fundraising model, setbacks are inevitable. However, these challenges should not be viewed as failures but as valuable learning opportunities. By embracing this mindset, you foster a culture where experimentation is encouraged, and every experience—whether successful or not—contributes to growth and improvement.

Flexibility and the ability to learn from feedback are not just beneficial traits in human-centered fundraising; they are essential components of a successful strategy. By embracing these principles, you ensure that your approach remains responsive, effective, and truly centered on the needs and perspectives of all stakeholders involved.

Practical Checklist for Immediate Action

Here are practical steps you can take right now:

- Calculate your overall donor retention rate and share it with your board.
- Segment your donors by giving program and calculate retention for deeper insights.
- Map the donor journey and identify one transactional practice to stop.
- Pilot one relational initiative (e.g., donor thank-you calls, story-based communications).
- Use AI tools to segment donors and personalize outreach, if possible.
- Gather and act on donor feedback about their experience.
- Repeat the process for volunteers and community advocates.

Ethical Considerations in Human-Centered Fundraising

As we embrace a human-centered approach to fundraising, it's crucial to address the ethical considerations that arise. Fundraising that seeks donations with misleading facts, omitting the truth, exaggerating information, or using any other dishonest tactic is unethical. Let's explore some key ethical considerations:

Transparency and Honesty

Be transparent about how donations are used and the impact they create. Provide clear, accurate information to donors and stakeholders about your organization's finances, programs, and outcomes.

Balancing Donor Wishes with Community Needs

While it's important to respect donor intentions, ensure that your fundraising efforts primarily serve the needs of your beneficiaries and align with your mission. Be prepared to have difficult conversations with donors when their wishes conflict with community needs or organizational values. Assume good intent and engage in respectful dialogue.

Protecting Beneficiary Dignity

In your storytelling and impact reporting, always prioritize the dignity and privacy of those you serve. Obtain informed consent before sharing personal stories or images and avoid sensationalism or exploitation of marginalized populations. Do not re-enforce negative stereotypes of people or communities.

Responsible Use of Data

As you leverage technology and data analytics in your human-centered approach, ensure that you have robust data protection policies in place. Be transparent about how you collect, use, and store donor, volunteer, and beneficiary data, and give individuals control over their personal information. Of course, comply with all rules and regulations associated with privacy and personal information.

Leveraging Digital and Social Media

In today's digital age, incorporating online strategies is crucial for effective human-centered fundraising. Here's how to leverage digital and social media:

Optimizing Your Website

Your website is often the first point of contact for potential donors and community members. Ensure it's mobile-responsive, easy to navigate, and clearly communicates your mission and impact. Streamline your donation process to make it as simple and user-friendly as possible.

Social Media Engagement

Use social media platforms to share impact stories, build relationships, and drive traffic to your donation pages. Engage with your followers authentically, responding to comments and messages promptly. Consider using live video features to give behind-the-scenes glimpses of your work or host Q&A sessions with staff and beneficiaries.

Email Marketing

Segment your email list and personalize campaigns to engage donors with targeted, emotionally resonant appeals. Use email to share regular updates, impact stories, and calls to action.

Virtual Events

Host virtual events like webinars, online auctions, or virtual tours to engage supporters who may not be able to attend in-person events. These can be cost-effective ways to reach a broader audience and create meaningful connections.

Measuring and Communicating Impact

In a human-centered fundraising approach, measuring and communicating impact goes beyond traditional financial metrics. It's about capturing the full spectrum of change your organization creates in the lives of individuals and communities.

Developing a Comprehensive Impact Framework

Create an impact framework that incorporates both quantitative and qualitative measures. This might include:

- Traditional fundraising metrics (e.g., funds raised, donor retention rates, lifetime value)
- Program outcomes (e.g., number of beneficiaries served, specific improvements in their lives)
- Stakeholder satisfaction scores (for donors, volunteers, staff, and beneficiaries)
- Community-level indicators (e.g., changes in local poverty rates, education outcomes)
- Organizational health metrics (e.g., staff retention, volunteer engagement)

Collecting Meaningful Data

Implement systems to regularly collect data across your impact framework. This might involve:

- Surveys and feedback forms
- In-depth interviews with beneficiaries and community members
- Social media sentiment analysis
- Program evaluation tools
- Financial and operational data tracking

Telling Impactful Stories

While data is crucial, stories bring your impact to life. Develop a storytelling strategy that:

- Highlights individual beneficiary experiences with dignity, respect, and consent
- Showcases community-level changes
- Demonstrates the ripple effects of your work
- Includes donor and volunteer perspectives

Ensure all storytelling is ethical, obtaining proper consent and protecting individuals' dignity.

Creating Engaging Impact Reports

Move beyond traditional annual reports to create engaging, multi-media impact communications.

Consider:

- Interactive digital reports with embedded videos and infographics
- Regular impact updates via email or social media
- Personalized impact statements for major donors
- Community impact presentations or events

Engaging Stakeholders in Impact Assessment

Involve your stakeholders in the process of defining and measuring impact. This might include:

- Participatory evaluation sessions with beneficiaries
- Donor surveys on what impact metrics matter most to them
- Staff and volunteer input on defining success

By involving stakeholders, you ensure your impact measurement truly reflects what matters to your community.

Sector-Specific Considerations

While the principles of human-centered fundraising apply across the non-profit sector, implementation may vary based on your specific field. Here are some considerations for different types of organizations:

Health Nonprofits

- Focus on patient stories and long-term health outcomes with permission
- Engage medical professionals in your fundraising efforts
- Consider the ethical implications of sharing health information

Environmental Organizations

- Use visual storytelling to showcase environmental changes
- Engage supporters in citizen science initiatives
- Highlight the interconnectedness of environmental and human wellbeing

Arts Institutions

- Demonstrate the broader community impact of arts programs
- Engage artists and performers in your fundraising efforts
- Use creative, artistic approaches in your communications

Education Nonprofits

- Showcase long-term student success stories
- Engage alumni in mentoring and fundraising
- Demonstrate the ripple effects of education on communities

Case Study: The Transformation of Hope Community Services

To illustrate the power of this journey, let's look at the experience of Hope Community Services, a mid-sized nonprofit serving homeless youth in Seattle.

When new Executive Director, Maria Chen, joined Hope Community Services in 2022, she found an organization struggling with donor attrition and staff burnout. The fundraising team was focused on transactional relationships, sending out generic appeals and thank you letters. Community members and youth served by the organization felt disconnected from decision-making processes.

Maria decided to embark on a human-centered fundraising journey. Here's how they applied the steps we've discussed:

- **Assessment:** Maria conducted a thorough audit of fundraising practices and gathered feedback from donors, staff, youth, and community members.

- **Strategy Development:** Based on this feedback, Hope developed a new strategy focused on building long-term relationships with donors and involving youth and community members in program design.
- **Infrastructure Building:** The organization invested in a new CRM system to better track donor interactions and preferences. They also provided staff training in relationship-based fundraising and community facilitation.
- **Overcoming Challenges:** When some board members expressed concern about the cost of the new approach, Maria organized a retreat where youth shared their experiences directly with the board. This powerful interaction helped secure buy-in for the changes.
- **Implementation and Iteration:** Hope rolled out their new approach in phases, starting with a pilot group of donors. They used feedback from this group to refine their strategies before scaling up.

The results have been transformative. Two years into their journey:

- Donor retention rates have increased by 25%
- Average gift sizes have grown by 15%
- A new youth advisory board is actively shaping program decisions
- Staff turnover has decreased by 30%
- Most importantly, the number of youth successfully transitioning out of homelessness has increased by 40%

Maria attributes these successes to the shift toward a more human-centered approach. "By putting people—our donors, our youth, our staff, and our community—at the center of everything we do, we've created a more vibrant, effective, and impactful organization," she says.

The Future of Human-Centered Fundraising

As we look to the future, human-centered fundraising will continue to evolve. It's essential to look ahead and consider how this model will evolve. The strategies we've discussed—assessing current practices, developing a human-centered vision, and embracing flexibility—are foundational. Now, let's examine some trends that will shape the future of fundraising.

Emerging Trends

- **Increased Use of AI and Machine Learning:** AI can help personalize donor experiences by analyzing donor behavior and preferences, allowing for more targeted and meaningful interactions. For example, AI-driven systems can automate personalized thank-you messages or suggest relevant giving opportunities based on a donor's history.
- **Greater Emphasis on Systemic Issues:** This trend involves moving beyond immediate needs to address the root causes of social problems. It might involve partnering with other organizations to create collective impact initiatives that tackle systemic issues like poverty or inequality.
- **More Collaborative Approaches:** Collective impact initiatives bring together multiple stakeholders to achieve common goals. This collaborative approach can enhance the effectiveness of fundraising efforts by leveraging diverse perspectives and resources.
- **Growing Focus on Long-Term Sustainability and Resilience:** As organizations face increasing uncertainty, focusing on long-term sustainability ensures that fundraising efforts are not just effective today but also viable in the future. This might involve diversifying revenue streams or building strong relationships with donors who can provide consistent support.

Preparing for the Future

To stay ahead of these trends, consider the following strategies:

- **Invest in Technology:** Explore AI tools that can enhance donor engagement and personalize communications.
- **Engage in Collective Impact:** Look for opportunities to collaborate with other organizations on systemic issues.
- **Prioritize Sustainability:** Develop strategies to ensure long-term financial stability, such as diversifying your donor base or creating endowments.

Reflection and Action

As you look to the future, ask yourself:

- How can these trends enhance our human-centered approach? What steps can we take today to prepare for these changes?
- By staying attuned to these trends while remaining grounded in human-centered principles, you can ensure your fundraising efforts remain effective and impactful.

Key Takeaways and Action Steps

As we conclude our exploration of the hero's journey toward human-centered fundraising, let's recap the key lessons and outline some immediate steps you can take:

Key Takeaways

- Human-centered community engagement and fundraising are a journey, not a destination. It requires ongoing commitment and adaptation.
- Engage all stakeholders—donors, community members, staff, and beneficiaries—in the process of change.
- Balance quantitative metrics with qualitative feedback to measure the full impact of your approach.
- Invest in technology and skills that enhance, rather than replace, human connections.
- Foster a culture of empathy, learning, and agility to support your human-centered approach.
- Be prepared to face challenges but remember that each obstacle is an opportunity for growth and improvement.

Action Steps

- Conduct a mini audit of your current fundraising practices. Identify one area where you could immediately inject more human-centered principles.
- Schedule conversations with a diverse group of stakeholders (donors, community members, staff, beneficiaries) to gather their perspectives on your current approach.

- Map out the journey of one key stakeholder group (e.g., first-time donors or monthly givers) and brainstorm ways to make each touchpoint more meaningful and impactful.
- Identify one new metric you could start tracking to measure the human impact of your fundraising efforts.
- Plan a team discussion or workshop to explore how you can foster a more empathetic and learning-oriented culture in your fundraising work.

Answering the Call

As we conclude our exploration of the hero's journey in implementing a human-centered fundraising approach, it's clear that the path forward is not just about adopting new strategies but also about measuring and communicating the impact of these efforts. The journey doesn't end with the successful implementation of a human-centered model; it continues with the critical task of evaluating its effectiveness, continuous improvement, and sharing that story with the world.

In Chapter 12, "Measuring Impact: Metrics for a New Era of Fundraising," we will delve into the metrics and KPIs that accurately reflect the success of human-centered fundraising. We'll explore how to track and communicate impact to donors and the community, ensuring that your organization's story of change resonates deeply with those who matter most. By mastering these skills, you'll not only demonstrate the value of your human-centered approach but also inspire continued support and collaboration from your stakeholders, propelling your organization toward even greater heights of impact and success.

By putting people at the center of our fundraising efforts—whether they're donors, beneficiaries, staff, or community members—we create a more inclusive, effective, and ultimately more impactful approach to philanthropy.

As you embark on your own hero's journey toward human-centered fundraising, remember that you're not alone. You are part of a growing movement of fundraisers and nonprofit leaders who are reimagining what's possible in our field.

The challenges we face in our communities are complex and often daunting. But by embracing a human-centered approach, we can unlock new levels of creativity, collaboration, and impact. We can create a future where every nonprofit thrives, every mission is fully funded, and every community has the support it needs to flourish.

Your journey starts now. Take that first step, embrace the challenges and opportunities ahead, and let your human-centered fundraising adventure begin. Together, we can transform not only our organizations but the entire landscape of philanthropy.

The world is waiting for heroes like you. Will you answer the call?

10 | AI: The Responsible and Beneficial Sidekick in Human–Centered Fundraising

> "I do not believe that AI will replace fundraisers, but fundraisers
> who use AI will replace those that don't."
> —Nathan Chappell, MBA, MNA, CFRE, Author, AI Inventor,
> Co-Founder of Fundraising.AI

Imagine you're a fundraiser, standing at the edge of a vast digital landscape. In one hand, you hold the warm, personal connections you've cultivated with donors over years. In the other, a powerful AI tool promising to revolutionize your fundraising efforts. How do you bridge these two worlds without losing the essence of what makes fundraising truly impactful—the human touch?

Integrating AI as Essential, Not Optional

AI is no longer a luxury for nonprofits—it's a necessity. In today's digital-first environment, organizations that fail to embrace AI risk falling behind. Far from replacing the human connection at the heart of fundraising, the right AI tools can actually enhance it—offloading time-consuming tasks and giving fundraisers more space to focus on the relationships that drive their mission forward.

The nonprofit sector stands at a pivotal moment: doing things the same way will not meet the humanitarian demands of this or future generations. Amid fractured societies, declining civic engagement, and escalating humanitarian crises, the need for nonprofit services and innovation has never been greater. Embracing AI-driven innovation is not a luxury, but a necessity. Organizations that fail to adapt risk falling behind, leading to a less diverse and less effective sector. AI is not just a tool for fundraising—it is reshaping every aspect of nonprofit work, from operations and program delivery to marketing and impact measurement. The organizations that thrive will be those that use AI to amplify their human-centered approach and mission.

Welcome to the new frontier of fundraising, where artificial intelligence isn't just a buzzword, but a potential game-changer for nonprofits worldwide. As we embark on this journey together, remember: AI isn't here to replace you. It's here to be your sidekick, enhancing your superpowers and helping you save the day (and your sanity) in the complex world of nonprofit fundraising.

The Generosity Crisis: A Sobering Reality

In many developed nations, the number of people donating or volunteering with nonprofits has seen systemic declines. For example, the percentage of US households giving to nonprofits fell from 66% in 2000 to less than 50% by

> *2018. This "dollars up, donors down" trend means fewer donors are giving more, creating a fragile system vulnerable to economic shifts. At the same time, today's donors—especially younger generations—expect personalized engagement and transparent, data-driven impact reporting. Meeting these expectations requires new approaches, and AI is uniquely positioned to help nonprofits rebuild trust and engagement at scale.*

In this chapter, we'll explore how AI can amplify your human-centered fundraising approach, turning you into the fundraising hero your cause deserves. We'll navigate the ethical considerations, uncover practical strategies for leveraging AI in your major gift programs, and learn how to maintain that crucial human touch in an increasingly digital world.

Here's what you can expect to learn:

- How AI can enhance rather than replace human connection in fundraising
- The ethical considerations and how to develop a responsible AI integration strategy
- Practical ways to leverage AI in major gift programs
- Steps to develop an AI ethical use policy for your organization
- Strategies for maintaining the human touch in an AI-enhanced fundraising landscape
- Real-world examples and case studies of successful AI implementation in fundraising
- Future trends in AI and fundraising

So, strap in, future fundraising superheroes—it's time to discover how AI can help us create a brighter, more funded future for all.

Demystifying AI in Fundraising: Your New Superpower

Let's start by addressing the elephant in the room—the fear that AI will somehow make fundraising cold and impersonal. Nothing could be further from the truth. When used correctly, AI is like having a brilliant research assistant, a meticulous taskmaster, a tireless data analyst, and an insightful strategist all rolled into one.

AI in fundraising isn't about replacing human interaction; it's about enhancing it. Think of it as your fundraising utility belt, equipped with tools to make your job easier and more effective. Here's how:

- **Enhanced Donor Insights:** AI can analyze vast amounts of data to uncover patterns and preferences you might miss. It's like having X-ray vision into your donor database, revealing hidden gems— donors with high giving potential who haven't been on your radar. AI can also identify and alert you to donors at risk of lapsing, long before you would typically know.
- **Personalized Communication:** AI can help tailor your messages to resonate with individual donors, ensuring your communications hit the mark every time. This personal touch is crucial in building strong relationships.
- **Predictive Analytics:** By analyzing past giving patterns, AI can help predict future donor behavior, allowing you to focus your efforts where they're most likely to succeed.
- **Efficient Administration:** AI can automate routine tasks, freeing you up to do what you do best—building relationships and inspiring generosity.

Precision Philanthropy and Predictive Analytics

AI enables nonprofits to gain predictive insights into donor behavior, enhancing donor retention and personalizing outreach. Predictive analytics can identify high-potential donors, forecast donation cycles, and target personalized outreach, leading to increased donations and loyalty. AI models can continuously refine predictions based on new donor interactions, improving accuracy over time.

Streamlining Fundraising with Automation

AI-powered automation can handle repetitive tasks like managing donor records, sending follow-up emails, and generating reports. Automation ensures consistent communication, reduces human error, and frees up staff to focus on strategic activities. AI can also automate donor onboarding journeys, recurring donation reminders, and impact reporting, further increasing efficiency.

AI's value for nonprofits extends well beyond fundraising. Key benefits include:

- Automating routine tasks, freeing staff for more strategic work
- Personalizing stakeholder engagement at scale
- Optimizing resource allocation and program delivery
- Enhancing impact measurement and real-time reporting
- Improving decision-making with predictive analytics
- Predicting trends and needs in the communities you serve

These efficiencies enable nonprofits to focus more on creative, mission-critical tasks, thereby amplifying their ability to create a lasting impact.

Recent survey data from the 2024 Momentum Nonprofit Productivity Report reveals that fundraisers spend the majority of their time on donor identification and drafting outreach emails-tasks that AI can dramatically expedite. For instance, 37% of a fundraiser's time is spent identifying who to reach out to and 35% on drafting emails, with major gift officers often spending 30–60 minutes per email. This not only limits time for relationship-building but also contributes to burnout and turnover. Notably, 76% of fundraisers agree that reducing manual tasks would increase their job satisfaction, and 69% believe AI tools could help achieve this.

AI for More Time with Donors:

When leveraged thoughtfully, AI automates repetitive tasks like drafting emails, creating reports, and generating content. This means more time for what matters most: building authentic relationships with your donors.

Myths and Realities of AI in Fundraising

Myth: AI will Replace Fundraisers

Reality: AI augments human connection by automating routine tasks, allowing staff to focus on building relationships and strategic work.

Myth: AI Is Only for Large Organizations

Reality: Today's cloud-based and no-code AI tools make advanced technology accessible to nonprofits of all sizes.

Myth: AI Is Infallible

Reality: AI is only as good as the data and oversight behind it. Human review is always essential. Bias in AI is prevalent and hallucinations occur. Oversight is critical.

Think of AI as "augmented intelligence"—a partner that enhances your capabilities, not a competitor. The synergy between AI and human expertise enables nonprofits to reach new heights in serving their mission.

While a strong majority (82%) of fundraisers are now comfortable using AI for donor outreach, many remain cautious about AI's role in personalizing communications. The Momentum report found that 63% of respondents are unsure or uncomfortable with AI-generated personalized messages, concerned they may feel less authentic. This highlights the importance of pairing AI with human oversight—using AI to draft and personalize at scale but always reviewing for authenticity and nuance before sending.

Remember, AI is not meant to replace your intuition or experience. It's a tool to augment your skills, allowing you to work smarter, not harder.

The Ethical Compass: Navigating AI in Nonprofit Waters

As Spiderman's Uncle Ben once told Peter Parker, "With great power comes great responsibility." The same holds true for AI in fundraising. While the potential benefits are enormous, it's crucial to approach AI integration with a strong ethical framework. Creating a comprehensive AI ethics policy is like crafting a mission statement for your AI initiatives. It sets the tone for how your organization will use AI responsibly and ethically. Here's a step-by-step guide to developing your AI ethics policy:

- **Define Your AI Purpose:** Clearly articulate why you're implementing AI and how it aligns with your mission.
- **Establish Transparency:** Commit to being open about your use of AI with donors and stakeholders.
- **Ensure Data Privacy and Security:** Outline strict protocols for protecting donor information.

- **Address Bias and Fairness:** Implement measures to identify and mitigate potential biases in AI algorithms.
- **Set Accountability Measures:** Designate roles and responsibilities for overseeing AI use and addressing concerns.
- **Plan for Continuous Review:** Schedule regular assessments of your AI practices to ensure they remain ethical and effective.
- **Create an AI Governance Policy:** Begin your AI journey by establishing a governance policy. This living document should define acceptable AI tools and uses, align with your organizational values, and be reviewed regularly as technology evolves. Consider using templates from trusted sources like *Fundraising.AI*.

Responsible AI use means more than compliance—it requires explainable AI (XAI), privacy-preserving approaches (like federated learning), and regular ethical audits. Involve diverse stakeholders in AI governance to ensure alignment with your mission and values. As guardians of public trust, nonprofits must prioritize beneficial and transparent AI utilization while safeguarding the long-term sustainability of the sector.

When selecting AI tools, be mindful of privacy. Paid versions of AI tools often provide enhanced data protection, which is critical when handling sensitive donor information. Prioritize these options to maintain donor trust and ensure compliance with privacy standards.

Dr. Emily Chang, an AI ethics researcher at Stanford University, emphasizes the importance of transparency in AI use: "Nonprofits have a unique responsibility when it comes to AI ethics. Their donors trust them with not just their money but their data and their values. Being transparent about how AI is used to further the mission can actually deepen donor trust and engagement."

In a 2024 national survey of over 1,000 US donors, Nathan Chappell and Cherian Koshy uncovered important insights into donor perceptions of artificial intelligence (AI) in the nonprofit sector. Their research revealed that while more than 80% of donors are somewhat or very familiar with AI, trust and transparency remain the defining factors in whether donors feel comfortable with its use. A remarkable 93% of respondents said it is important for nonprofits to be open about how AI is used in their operations, especially when it involves donor data and personalization.

The findings also show that while donors value efficiency and impact measurement—areas where AI can be particularly effective—many are uneasy about its role in personalizing outreach or analyzing giving behaviors without clear consent. Nearly one in three donors said they would be less likely to give if they discovered a nonprofit was using AI without transparency. This discomfort was particularly pronounced among older donors, while younger and higher-income donors were generally more open to AI integration.

Chappell and Koshy's research underscores that donors aren't anti-AI; rather, they are pro-trust. Nonprofits should clearly communicate how AI supports, rather than replaces, human decision-making. Sharing examples of how AI improves efficiency or strengthens stewardship can reassure donors, as can offering opt-in or opt-out options for AI-driven personalization. Ultimately, transparency about AI usage is not just good ethics—it's a key strategy for maintaining donor confidence in a rapidly evolving digital landscape.

The takeaway? As fundraising professionals, our work is built on trust—and that trust can be shaken if donors feel we're using technology in ways that aren't transparent.

If your organization is using AI—whether it's to identify potential major donors, personalize thank-you emails, or analyze which appeals are most effective—it's important to tell donors. Not in a scary or technical way, but with clear, human-centered language.

For example:

- "We use smart tools to help us thank donors faster and more personally."
- "AI helps us match your giving with the programs you care most about."
- "We use technology to be efficient and direct more resources to the mission."

Being open about how AI supports (but doesn't replace) the human relationships at the heart of fundraising builds credibility and confidence.

Disclosing AI use isn't just ethical—it's smart stewardship. Donors will appreciate your honesty, especially when they see how it helps your team work more efficiently and serve the mission more effectively.

Case Study: St. John Fisher University's AI-Powered Fundraising Success

St. John Fisher University provides an excellent example of how to ethically and effectively integrate AI into fundraising efforts. The university leveraged AI tools to enhance its donor outreach and hit aggressive giving goals, all while maintaining a strong ethical framework.

Key takeaways from their success:

- They used AI to reduce administrative tasks for gift officers, freeing up time for meaningful donor connections.
- Their AI-driven ambassador program saw a 91% growth rate in membership.
- 66% of all unrestricted fundraising dollars through the annual fund were raised by AI-engaged ambassadors.
- They exceeded their $100 million campaign goal ahead of schedule, reaching $102 million by December 2023.

St. John Fisher's success demonstrates that when AI is used ethically and strategically, it can significantly amplify fundraising efforts without compromising personal relationships or donor trust.

AI in Action: Practical Strategies for Major Gift Programs

Now that we've laid the ethical groundwork, let's explore how AI can supercharge your major gift programs. Here are some practical strategies to implement:

Smarter Prospect Research

AI can analyze a vast array of data points to identify potential major donors you might have overlooked. It can consider factors like giving history, wealth indicators, social media engagement, and even news mentions to create a more comprehensive donor profile.

Strategy: Use AI-powered tools to conduct an initial screening of your donor database. This can help you identify "hidden gems"—donors with high giving potential who haven't been on your radar.

Personalized Donor Journeys

AI can help map out individualized donor journeys, suggesting the right touchpoints at the right times based on a donor's behavior and preferences.

Strategy: Implement an AI-driven donor journey mapping tool. Use it to create personalized cultivation plans for each major gift prospect, ensuring every interaction moves them closer to a significant gift.

Predictive Giving Analysis

By analyzing historical giving data, AI can predict when a donor is most likely to give and at what level.

Strategy: Use AI predictive models to time your major gift solicitations. This can help you approach donors when they're most receptive and with an ask amount that aligns with their giving capacity.

Enhanced Proposal Writing

While the personal touch is crucial in proposal writing, AI can assist by providing data-driven insights and even helping to draft initial versions.

Strategy: Use AI writing tools to create first drafts of proposals, then personalize and refine them based on your knowledge of the donor. This can save time while ensuring your proposals are data-informed and tailored to each prospect.

Automated Follow-ups

AI can help you stay on top of your follow-up game by suggesting timely check-ins based on donor interactions.

Strategy: Implement an AI-powered CRM that prompts you with follow-up reminders and suggests talking points based on previous interactions and donor interests.

Practical AI Use Cases in Fundraising

- Generative AI can create compelling stories, personalized videos, and targeted campaigns to engage donors effectively

- Generating customized donor messages and thank-you notes
- Automating reports and meeting summaries
- Creating blog posts, social media content, and fundraising appeals
- Drafting first versions of proposals for refinement

Platforms like Momentum exemplify how AI can streamline nonprofit workflows. Their AI-powered Donor Engagement platform enables fundraisers to:

- Create and update custom donor plans automatically
- Prioritize outreach with daily reminders
- Generate hyper-personalized communications in the fundraiser's own style
- Sync CRM data in real time, eliminating manual entry

These features address the most time-consuming aspects of fundraising, allowing staff to focus on building relationships and driving impact.

Checklist for AI Adoption in Fundraising

- **Define Clear Goals:** Establish specific objectives for AI adoption, such as improving donor retention or campaign efficiency.
- **Engage Leadership and Stakeholders:** Secure buy-in from leadership and key stakeholders to ensure resource allocation and cultural support.
- **Invest in Staff Training:** Provide training to build confidence and understanding of AI tools.
- **Leverage Existing Tools:** Use proven AI platforms tailored for nonprofits to reduce complexity and cost.
- **Monitor and Evaluate Progress:** Regularly assess AI initiatives to refine strategies and maximize impact.

Best Practice:

AI-generated content is increasingly accurate but always review and fact-check before sending to donors or publishing. Human oversight ensures accuracy and maintains trust.

Remember, these AI-powered strategies are meant to enhance, not replace, your personal approach to major gift fundraising. The goal is to use AI to work smarter, allowing you more time to focus on building those crucial donor relationships.

Real-World Example: The Nature Conservancy's AI-Powered Donor Segmentation

The Nature Conservancy, a global environmental organization, used AI to analyze its donor database and create more nuanced donor segments. By incorporating factors like giving history, engagement levels, and areas of interest, they were able to create highly personalized communication strategies for each segment. The result? A 3% increase in donor retention and a 5% boost in average gift size within the first year of implementation.

Additionally, the **American Red Cross** has also seen success with AI by using it to analyze donor behavior and tailor their appeals to specific segments, resulting in a significant increase in donations during disaster relief campaigns.

AI for Volunteer Engagement and Management

AI's benefits extend far beyond fundraising. In volunteer management, predictive AI can anticipate future volunteer needs, flag volunteers at risk of disengagement, and optimize allocation based on historical data. Generative AI enables nonprofits to craft tailored messages, training content, and event invitations based on individual volunteer preferences and history. AI can personalize recognition efforts, such as thank-you messages or public acknowledgments, fostering a deeper sense of belonging and commitment.

Automation AI can handle repetitive tasks like scheduling shifts, managing communication, and generating reports. AI-powered tools can automate onboarding, send reminders, and track volunteer hours, freeing staff to focus on strategic initiatives. Automated follow-ups (e.g., thank-you notes and impact summaries) ensure consistent communication and enhance volunteer satisfaction.

Recommendations for AI in Volunteer Management

- **Identify Specific Pain Points:** Focus on areas where AI can address challenges, such as recruitment or retention.

- **Collaborate with Peers and Experts:** Share best practices and insights with other nonprofits and AI professionals.
- **Allocate Budget for Maintenance:** Plan for ongoing updates and support to ensure AI tools remain effective.
- **Monitor AI Performance:** Regularly evaluate AI tools to refine strategies and improve outcomes.
- **Encourage Open Communication:** Foster a culture where staff and volunteers can provide feedback on AI implementations.

Maintaining the Human Touch in an AI-Enhanced Fundraising Landscape

As we integrate AI into our fundraising strategies, it's crucial to remember that AI is meant to augment, not replace, human interaction. The goal is to use AI to work smarter, allowing you more time to focus on building those crucial donor relationships. Here are some strategies to maintain the human touch:

- **Personalize Communications:** While AI can help tailor messages, ensure that every communication still reflects your personal connection with the donor.
- **Engage in Meaningful Interactions:** Use AI to free up time for face-to-face meetings, phone calls, and handwritten notes—actions that show donors they're valued.
- **Tell Compelling Stories:** AI can help identify the right stories to share, but it's your passion and authenticity that bring those stories to life.

AI Tools and Platforms for Nonprofits

Here's a brief overview of some popular AI tools and platforms that nonprofits can leverage:

- **Virtuous:** Virtuous combines donor management, marketing automation, volunteer management, and advanced analytics into a single, user-friendly system. This holistic approach enables organizations to streamline their operations, personalize donor engagement, and make data-driven decisions to maximize their social impact.

- **DonorSearch:** DonorSearch offers industry-leading AI and machine learning solutions specifically tailored for nonprofits. Its DonorSearch Ai platform leverages predictive and generative AI to identify high-impact donors, segment prospects with high accuracy, and personalize outreach—enabling organizations to increase response rates, average gift size, and donor retention significantly.
- **Kindsight:** Kindsight's fundraising intelligence platform natively integrates big data, AI, and automation into a single, enterprise-grade CRM. Kindsight's platform combines real-time donor data, wealth insights, and AI-powered content creation, enabling nonprofits to identify and engage the right donors at the right time—every time.
- **Gravyty:** Gravyty's unique blend of AI technology, automation, and community engagement tools empowers nonprofits to maximize their social impact through smarter, more personal, and more efficient fundraising.
- **Salesforce Einstein:** An AI layer that can be added to Salesforce's Nonprofit Cloud, offering predictive analytics and automated insights.
- **Bloomerang:** A donor management software that uses AI to provide donor retention suggestions and predict donor churn.
- **GiveSmart:** An AI-powered platform for event management and mobile bidding, which can help optimize fundraising events.
- **Avid.AI:** An AI-powered fundraising operating system that connects your nonprofit's CRM, email, ad platforms, and donation tools—turning donor data into daily priorities, automated campaigns, smart segmentation, and real-time, actionable fundraising insights

Start by exploring a few AI tools, then commit to the ones that best fit your organization's needs. Avoid the temptation to constantly switch; instead, focus on mastering one or two tools that integrate well with your daily work. Generative AI platforms like ChatGPT, Claude, Copilot, and Gemini are excellent starting points for content creation, donor communications, and automating reports.

Remember to thoroughly research and test any tool before fully implementing it in your fundraising strategy. It's also crucial to explore and engage data privacy capabilities to the fullest extent.

Common Challenges and Solutions in AI Implementation

While AI offers tremendous potential, nonprofits often face challenges when implementing these technologies. Here are some common hurdles and strategies to overcome them:

Budget Constraints

Challenge: Many nonprofits operate on tight budgets, making it difficult to invest in AI technologies.

Solution: Start small with free or low-cost AI tools. Gradually build a case for more investment by demonstrating ROI on these initial efforts.

Staff Resistance

Challenge: Team members may be hesitant to adopt new technologies, fearing job displacement or a steep learning curve.

Solution: Provide comprehensive training and emphasize how AI will enhance, not replace their roles. Involve staff in the AI implementation process to build buy-in.

Data Quality Issues

Challenge: AI systems require high-quality, consistent data to function effectively.

Solution: Conduct a thorough data audit and cleaning process before implementing AI. Establish ongoing data management protocols to maintain data quality and integrity over time.

Data Privacy Concerns

Challenge: Ensuring data privacy in cloud-based AI systems is crucial.

Solution: Implement robust data encryption and access controls. Regularly review cloud service agreements to ensure they meet your privacy standards.

Managing Donor Perceptions

Challenge: Donors may have concerns about AI use, so it's important to manage their perceptions.

Solution: Be transparent about AI use and its benefits. Highlight how AI helps personalize their experience and supports the mission.

Ethical Concerns

Challenge: Stakeholders may have concerns about the ethical implications of using AI in fundraising.

Solution: Develop and communicate a clear AI ethics policy. Be transparent with donors about how you're using AI and the benefits it brings to your mission.

Integration with Existing Systems

Challenge: AI tools may not easily integrate with your current technology stack.

Solution: Prioritize AI solutions that offer APIs or native integrations with your existing systems. Consider working with IT consultants to ensure smooth integration.

Leadership

Challenge: Executive leadership's lack of understanding of AI, combined with general nonprofit risk aversion, results in organizations taking a wait-and-see approach to AI adoption, falling behind the technology curve.

Solution: Create a task force to develop an AI use policy to provide guardrails for the responsible and beneficial use of AI, define what you'd like to achieve with it, identify priority use cases to pilot AI technology at your organization, and start small.

Successful AI adoption hinges on comprehensive training and ongoing support. The Momentum report underscores that fundraisers are most effective with AI when they receive education on its use and have access to support services. When selecting AI solutions, prioritize platforms that offer robust onboarding and continuous learning opportunities for your team.

Maintaining the Human Touch in an AI-Enhanced Landscape

As we embrace AI in our fundraising efforts, it's crucial to remember that at its core, fundraising is about human connections. Here's how to ensure you're leveraging AI while keeping your fundraising efforts authentically human:

1. **Use AI for Insights, Not Decisions**
   Let AI crunch the numbers and provide insights, but always filter these through your human understanding and experience.

   Strategy: When AI suggests a particular approach or ask amount, consider it a data point, not a directive. Use your judgment and knowledge of the donor to make the final decision.
2. **Personalize Beyond Data**
   While AI can provide valuable donor insights, it's your personal touch that turns those insights into meaningful connections.

   Strategy: Use AI-generated donor profiles as a starting point, then enrich them with personal observations, shared experiences, and emotional connections that only human interaction can provide.
3. **Communicate Transparently**
   Be open with donors about how you're using AI to enhance your fundraising efforts. Most donors appreciate knowing that you're using innovative tools to maximize the impact of their gifts.

   Strategy: Include a section in your donor communications or on your website explaining how you use AI ethically to support your mission.
4. **Prioritize Face-to-Face Interactions**
   While AI can help with many aspects of fundraising, it can't replace the value of in-person meetings, especially for major gifts.

   Strategy: Use AI to help you prepare for donor meetings but prioritize face-to-face interactions for building relationships and making major gift asks.
5. **Inject Creativity and Emotion**
   AI can provide data and suggestions, but it's your human creativity and emotional intelligence that will truly inspire donors.

   Strategy: Use AI-generated insights as a springboard for creative storytelling. Craft narratives that not only present the facts but also touch the heart and inspire action.

The 2024 Momentum report reinforces that AI is most valuable when it acts as an accelerant for human expertise—not a substitute. AI can provide a first draft or template, but fundraisers' knowledge of donor relationships ensures communications remain authentic and meaningful. Think of AI as a time-saving collaborator, freeing you to focus on the creative and relational aspects that matter most.

Real-World Example: Charity: Water's Blend of AI and Human Touch

Charity: Water, known for its innovative approach to fundraising, uses AI to analyze donor behavior and personalize communications. However, they balance this with highly personal, creative campaigns. For instance, their "The Spring" monthly giving program uses AI for donor management but pairs it with personalized impact reports and handwritten thank-you notes. This blend of AI efficiency and human warmth has helped them achieve a 70% retention rate for their monthly donors, well above the nonprofit average.

Potential Risks and Mitigation Strategies

While AI offers numerous benefits, it's crucial to be aware of potential risks and how to mitigate them:

Data Breaches

Risk: AI systems often require access to sensitive donor data, increasing the risk of data breaches.

Mitigation: Implement robust cybersecurity measures, including encryption, regular security audits, and staff training on data protection best practices.

Algorithmic Bias

Risk: AI algorithms can inadvertently perpetuate or amplify biases present in their training data.

Mitigation: Regularly audit your AI systems for bias. Use diverse datasets for training and involve a diverse team in AI implementation and oversight.

Over-reliance on AI

Risk: There's a danger of becoming too dependent on AI, potentially neglecting human judgment and intuition.

Mitigation: Establish clear guidelines for when and how AI should be used. Encourage a culture where AI recommendations are always paired with human insight.

Donor Privacy Concerns

Risk: Donors may feel uncomfortable with the level of data analysis and personalization enabled by AI.

Mitigation: Be transparent about your AI use and data practices. Give donors control over their data and the option to opt out of AI-driven communications.

Technical Failures

Risk: AI systems can malfunction or make errors, potentially leading to miscommunications or strategic mistakes.

Mitigation: Always have human oversight of AI systems. Implement fail-safes and regular testing protocols to catch and correct errors quickly.

The Future of AI in Fundraising: Trends to Watch

As we look ahead, several exciting trends are emerging in the world of AI-powered fundraising. Staying informed about these developments can help you remain at the forefront of fundraising innovation:

- **Hyper-Personalization:** AI will enable even more granular personalization of donor communications and experiences. Imagine AI that can craft messages that resonate with a donor's personal values, communication style, and giving history.
- **AI-Driven Storytelling:** AI can help identify and craft compelling stories that resonate with donors, making fundraising appeals more effective.
- **Predictive Giving Models:** Advanced AI models will provide increasingly accurate predictions of donor behavior and giving potential. These models might incorporate external factors like economic indicators or social trends to refine predictions.
- **AI-Powered Chatbots:** More sophisticated AI chatbots will enhance donor engagement on websites and social media platforms.

These chatbots could handle complex queries, provide personalized giving suggestions, and even process donations.

- **Voice-Activated Giving:** As voice recognition technology improves, we may see a rise in voice-activated donation options. Donors might soon be able to make gifts simply by talking to their smart home devices.
- **AI-Assisted Donor Advisory Boards:** AI can assist in forming advisory boards by analyzing donor networks and identifying key influencers.
- **Blockchain and AI Integration:** The combination of blockchain technology and AI could revolutionize transparency and efficiency in nonprofit operations. This could lead to real-time impact tracking and automated, smart-contract-based fund distribution.
- **Virtual Reality for Immersive Experiences:** Virtual reality can create immersive experiences that bring donors closer to the cause, fostering deeper engagement and empathy.
- **Emotion AI:** Advances in emotion recognition AI could help fundraisers gauge donor sentiment more accurately, even in digital interactions. This could inform more empathetic and effective communication strategies.
- **AI-Driven Event Planning:** AI could optimize fundraising events by predicting attendance, suggesting optimal ticket prices, and even recommending the best date and venue based on historical data.

While these trends are exciting, remember that the key to successful fundraising will always be the human connection. Use these innovations to enhance, not replace, your personal approach to donor relationships.

Look for Trends Such As

- Generative AI for multimedia storytelling and content creation
- AI-powered chatbots for donor engagement
- Edge AI for field operations in resource-constrained environments
- Agentive AI (autonomous systems acting on behalf of users)
- Federated learning for privacy-preserving collaboration
- Emotion AI and voice-activated giving

These technologies will further personalize donor experiences, expand your organization's reach, and open new pathways for real-time decision-making and impact.

Expert Prediction

Woodrow Rosenbaum, Chief Data Officer at Giving Tuesday, offers this insight into the future of AI in fundraising: "In the next five years, we'll see AI not just as a tool for efficiency, but as a catalyst for innovation in giving. AI will help us uncover new giving behaviors and motivations, leading to entirely new fundraising models. The nonprofits that thrive will be those that use AI to amplify their human-centered approach, not replace it."

Embracing AI as Your Fundraising Sidekick

As we conclude our journey through the world of AI in human-centered fundraising, let's recap the key takeaways:

- AI is a powerful tool that can enhance, not replace, human fundraising efforts.
- Ethical considerations are paramount when implementing AI in nonprofit organizations.
- AI can significantly boost major gift programs through smarter prospect research, personalized donor journeys, and predictive giving analysis.
- Maintaining the human touch is crucial in an AI-enhanced fundraising landscape.
- Transparency about AI usage is key to building and sustaining donor trust.
- Staying informed about future AI trends can help you remain at the forefront of fundraising innovation.
- Understanding and mitigating potential risks is essential for responsible AI implementation.
- Real-world examples and case studies demonstrate the tangible benefits of AI in fundraising when used ethically and strategically.
- When facing a fundraising challenge or new initiative, ask, "How can AI help?"
- Encourage a culture of curiosity and experimentation within your team. Ask "what if" and be open to rethinking processes with AI in mind. This mindset is key to successful AI integration.

As a fundraiser, you are one of the heroes in your nonprofit's story. AI is simply your trusty sidekick, there to amplify your superpowers and help you achieve even greater impact. By embracing AI as an ethical, powerful tool in your fundraising efforts, you're not just keeping up with the times—you're leading the charge toward a future where every nonprofit thrives, every mission is fully funded, and every community has the support it needs to flourish.

As we return to the overarching theme of human-centered fundraising, it's clear that AI doesn't detract from this approach—it enhances it. By automating routine tasks and providing deeper insights, AI frees you to focus on what truly matters: building meaningful relationships with donors, understanding their passions, and connecting them with opportunities to make a difference. In this way, AI helps us create a more personalized, impactful, and ultimately more human fundraising experience.

Invest in AI fluency for your team. Provide ongoing training and encourage a culture of curiosity and adaptability to keep pace with technological change. AI fluency—the ability to understand, evaluate, and apply AI—is now a core competency for nonprofit professionals. This includes not just technical skills but also ethical awareness, creative problem-solving, and the ability to collaborate across roles.

Reflection Questions

To help you internalize the concepts we've covered and apply them to your unique context, consider the following questions:

- How could AI help address your organization's most pressing fundraising challenges?
- What aspects of your current fundraising process could benefit most from AI enhancement?
- How can you ensure that AI implementation aligns with your organization's values and mission?
- What steps can you take to maintain authentic, personal connections with donors while leveraging AI?
- How might AI change the role of fundraisers in your organization, and how can you prepare your team for these changes?
- How will we ensure transparency and ethical AI usage?

By thoughtfully considering these questions and taking action on the insights you've gained from this chapter, you'll be well-positioned to harness the power of AI while staying true to the human-centered approach that is at the heart of effective fundraising.

Key Takeaways and Action Steps

Key Takeaways

- **AI Is a Fundraising Necessity:** In the current digital era, integrating AI into fundraising isn't just an advantage—it's essential. Organizations that don't adapt risk being left behind in a rapidly changing landscape.
- **AI Amplifies, Not Replaces, the Human Touch:** The power of successful fundraising still originates from genuine, personal connections with donors. AI isn't a substitute for these relationships; instead, it enables fundraisers to spend more time nurturing them by automating tedious, repetitive tasks.
- **The Sector Stands at a Crossroads:** The world faces growing humanitarian needs, social divides, and decreased civic engagement. Nonprofits can no longer rely on old methods; innovation—especially through AI—is critical to meet present and future demands.
- **AI Drives Innovation Across Nonprofit Work:** From fundraising and marketing to operations and impact measurement, AI is transforming every corner of the nonprofit sector. Embracing these changes can lead to a more diverse, agile, and effective organization.

Action Steps

- **Adopt a Mindset of Urgency:** Treat AI adoption as a strategic urgency, not an optional add-on. Begin exploring the AI tools most relevant to your mission and fundraising goals.
- **Audit Your Time:** Identify which mundane or repetitive tasks can be automated. Free up bandwidth so your team can focus on building authentic, lasting donor relationships.
- **Prioritize Human-Centered AI:** Choose AI solutions that amplify your mission and put the human touch at the center. Use technology to tell richer stories, personalize outreach, and deepen engagement—not to depersonalize your cause.

- **Invest in Continuous Learning:** Keep your team (and yourself) informed about new AI developments. Encourage ongoing education, experimentation, and adaptation so your organization stays ahead of the curve.
- **Champion Innovation Organization Wide:** Help stakeholders understand that AI isn't just about fundraising—it impacts every aspect of your work. Bring program delivery, marketing, and operations into the conversation so everyone moves forward together.
- **Develop an AI Use Policy:** Form a cross-functional working group to draft an AI use policy that outlines ethical guidelines, data privacy standards, and donor transparency practices.
- **Ensure Transparency:** Create a clear, donor-friendly statement on your website or gift acknowledgment materials that explains how your organization uses AI—highlighting its role in supporting, not replacing, human relationships.

Embracing AI isn't about losing your organization's heart—it's about freeing your best people to do what they do best: connect, inspire, and drive real impact. Fundraising heroes aren't replaced by technology—AI is the tool that lets their superpowers shine.

Embracing the Future: From AI to Implementation

As we conclude this chapter on AI in human-centered fundraising, remember that AI is not just a tool; it's a partner that can help you achieve greater impact. By embracing AI responsibly and strategically, you can unlock new potential in your fundraising efforts.

Embracing AI transformation is an ongoing journey requiring curiosity, collaboration, and a willingness to learn from both successes and failures. Foster a culture of experimentation and cross-sector collaboration, and view AI adoption as a continual process rather than a one-time project.

In the next chapter, we'll explore how to navigate the challenges of implementing a human-centered fundraising model, including strategies for overcoming resistance to change and building a roadmap for successful implementation. We'll delve into common objections from stakeholders and provide actionable strategies for persuading leadership and board members to support this new approach. The journey ahead is exciting, and with AI by your side, you're ready to face any challenge that comes your way.

Challenges, Measurement, and the Future

These chapters address obstacles to change, methods for measuring success, and future trends, culminating in a call to action.

11 | Navigating the Challenges: Overcoming Resistance to Change

Imagine you're on a mission to save the world, but your team is stuck in the starting blocks. This is often the reality when introducing a new fundraising model, especially one as innovative as the human-centered approach. As a fundraiser or nonprofit leader, you know that shifting from traditional donor-centered or community-centered models to a blended approach can be daunting. Resistance to change is natural, but it doesn't have to be insurmountable.

In this chapter, you'll learn how to identify the roots of resistance, address common objections, and implement practical strategies to guide your organization through change. Along the way, you'll find real-world case studies, actionable toolkits, and proven techniques to help your team become champions of a more inclusive and impactful fundraising model. It's time to assemble your team of heroes and embark on a journey that will transform your fundraising efforts and create lasting impact in your community.

Understanding the Roots of Resistance

Before overcoming resistance, we need to understand it. Resistance to change often stems from fear—fear of failure, fear of losing control, or fear of the unknown. In nonprofits, this resistance can manifest as:

1. **Board Members' Concerns:** "Won't this alienate our major donors?"
2. **Leadership Hesitation:** "Can this new approach really deliver measurable results?"
3. **Donor Pushback:** "I thought I was your priority. Now you're focusing on the community?"
4. **Staff Overload:** "We're already stretched thin. How can we take on something new?"

Understanding these objections is the first step in addressing them. Resistance isn't inherently negative-it's an opportunity to engage in meaningful dialogue and build consensus.

Civil rights scholar John A. Powell reminds us that resistance is often rooted in a deeper need for belonging—the desire to be seen, valued, and included. When people feel excluded or "othered," fragmentation and polarization can take hold, making change feel threatening. By intentionally fostering belonging and practicing bridging—actively building connections across differences—organizations can reduce resistance and create an environment where all stakeholders feel valued and included.

Addressing Common Objections

When introducing a new fundraising model, stakeholders often have concerns. With the roots of resistance in mind, let's explore the most common objections and how to address them. Each objection presents an opportunity for dialogue, learning, and growth.

Objection: "This is too different from what we've always done."

- Emphasize the benefits of innovation and the potential for greater impact.
- Share case studies or success stories from similar organizations that have adopted human-centered fundraising models.
- Paint a vivid picture of success: "Imagine a future where every child in our community has access to quality education, where our donors feel like true partners in creating systemic change, and where our impact is measured not just in dollars raised, but in lives transformed."

Objection: "We don't have the resources or time to implement this."

- Highlight time-saving features and efficiency gains from the new model.
- Provide a phased implementation plan that aligns with existing resources and timelines.
- Consider using technology, such as AI, to streamline processes and reduce workload.
- Start small: Launch a community-driven crowdfunding campaign for a specific project. Set a modest goal, like raising $5,000 for a new community garden, with decisions on location and design made collaboratively with community members.
- Develop a "Human-Centered Fundraising Academy" for your staff and board. This could be a series of workshops covering topics like community engagement, inclusive decision-making, and measuring holistic impact.

Objection: "I'm not sure our donors will respond well to this approach."

■ Engage donors early in the process, involve them in storytelling, and demonstrate how this approach aligns with their values and goals. Use data and feedback from similar organizations to build confidence.

■ Host a series of "Change Cafés"—informal gatherings where stakeholders can voice concerns and explore the benefits of a human-centered approach. Make these interactive: use sticky notes for idea sharing or create a "concerns and solutions" wall.

■ Identify influential advocates within your organization. For example, if you have a board member who's also a community leader, she could be a powerful ally in persuading others. Equip her with talking points and encourage her to share her perspective at board meetings.

Objection: "What about the perceived risk of shifting from traditional models?"

■ Address this by presenting data on the success of blended models and involving leadership in risk assessment. Highlight how a human-centered approach can mitigate risks by fostering stronger community relationships and donor loyalty.

■ Share data and trends. Did you know that community-centric approaches can increase donor retention by up to 20%? Or that organizations involving beneficiaries in decision-making see a 30% increase in program effectiveness? Use these kinds of statistics to illustrate the potential impact.

■ Share success stories from organizations that have adopted human-centered models. For instance, the local food bank in Austin, Texas, saw a 50% increase in community engagement and a 25% boost in donations after involving community members in fundraising decisions.

Objection: "How will we allocate resources effectively?"

■ Develop a resource allocation plan that prioritizes key areas of the new model. Use tools like budget templates and resource mapping to ensure efficient use of resources.

■ Create multiple channels for input. Set up a "Change Suggestion Box" (both physical and digital), hold regular town halls, and use tools like Slido for anonymous Q&A sessions during meetings.

- Launch a monthly "Change Chronicle" newsletter, sharing updates, success stories, and lessons learned. Use a mix of formats—written updates, short videos, infographics—to keep it engaging.
- Be willing to adapt your approach based on feedback. If your pilot community fundraising event didn't work as planned, analyze why, adjust, and try again. Share this process transparently to show your commitment to learning and growth.
- Recognize contributions from all stakeholders. Host a "Changemaker Awards" ceremony, celebrating everyone from the board member who championed the new approach to the community member whose idea sparked a successful initiative.

Use metrics to track progress and share results widely. Create a simple dashboard showing increases in donor retention, community engagement, and program effectiveness.

Consistency in applying new approaches is as crucial as the strategies themselves. Organizations that prioritize steady follow-through are more likely to see sustained improvements in fundraising outcomes.

Maia McGill emphasizes the importance of addressing both the logistical and emotional roots of resistance. Hold space for concerns, practice active listening, and demonstrate empathy. Engage stakeholders early, provide training and resources, and celebrate incremental successes to build momentum. Leaders should model the desired changes, and organizations should remain flexible and responsive to feedback throughout the transition.

Addressing Technology and Resource Constraints

As nonprofits, we often face unique challenges with limited resources. Resource limitations are a reality for most nonprofits, but they don't have to stall progress. Here's how to move forward:

- **Cost-Effective Technology Solutions:**
  - Use free or low-cost project management tools like Trello or Asana.
  - Leverage social media for communication and engagement.
  - Consider open-source software for database management and donor tracking.

- **Implementing Change on a Budget:**
  - Prioritize high-impact, low-cost initiatives.
  - Seek pro-bono consulting services from local businesses or universities.
  - Create a "change champion" program where volunteers lead aspects of the transition.
- **Leveraging Volunteers:**
  - Develop a "Skills-Based Volunteering" program.
  - Create a "Change Ambassador" role for passionate volunteers.
  - Host "Hackathon for Change" events for collaborative problem-solving.

With these practical solutions in place, let's examine how real organizations have navigated similar challenges.

Case Studies: Overcoming Resistance

Let's look at some real-world examples of how a human-centered approach can overcome resistance to change:

Case Study 1:

A local environmental nonprofit faced resistance from long-time donors who were skeptical about shifting from a traditional donor-centered model. The organization addressed these concerns by involving donors in the storytelling process, highlighting how the new approach would increase community engagement and support for local environmental projects. Regular updates on impact and early wins reinforced the value of the human-centered model. As a result, donor retention increased, and new community partnerships were formed.

Case Study 2:

A healthcare organization used technology integration to streamline fundraising. By leveraging AI for data analysis, they personalized donor communications, leading to increased donations and reduced operational costs.

Toolkit of Techniques and Best Practices

To successfully implement a human-centered fundraising model, you need a versatile toolkit. Here are some techniques and best practices tailored for various nonprofit sectors:

- **Storytelling:** Use compelling narratives that resonate with both donors and the community. For example, a healthcare nonprofit might share stories of patients whose lives were improved through their services.
- **Team Building:** Assemble a diverse team with varied skills and perspectives. This ensures that your approach is well-rounded and adaptable to different sectors.
- **Technology Integration:** Leverage AI and digital tools to enhance efficiency and reach. For instance, AI can help personalize donor communications and streamline data analysis.
- **Feedback Loop:** Establish a continuous feedback loop with stakeholders to refine your approach and address concerns promptly.

Bridging and Belonging Practices

Add bridging practices to your toolkit: facilitate structured dialogues that bring together diverse stakeholders, encourage collaborative projects that cross traditional boundaries, and create spaces where all voices are heard. As outlined by John A. Powell, these approaches help counteract fragmentation and foster a sense of shared purpose.

Field-Tested Bridging Tools

Local leaders across the U.S. are overcoming polarization by creating opportunities for collaborative problem-solving—connecting youth across regions or convening interfaith leaders to strengthen community ties. These stories demonstrate that bridging divides is not only possible but essential for organizational and societal resilience.

Actionable Tools

- **Objection Handling Scripts:** Develop scripts that acknowledge concerns and offer solutions. For example, "I understand your concern about resource allocation. Let me show you how our phased plan ensures efficient use of resources."
- **Readiness Checklist:** Create a checklist to assess your organization's readiness for change, including factors like team buy-in and resource availability.
- **Communication Templates:** Use templates to ensure consistent messaging across all stakeholders, highlighting the benefits and impact of the new model.

Incorporating Donor Perspectives

Maintaining donor engagement during periods of change is crucial. Here's how:

- **Effective Communication:**
  - Create a "Donor Change Journey" map, outlining how the transition will enhance their impact.
  - Use personalized videos from leadership explaining the change and its benefits.
  - Offer "Behind the Scenes" webinars where donors can ask questions about the new approach.
- **Maintaining Trust:**
  - Implement a "Donor Advisory Board" to involve key supporters in the change process.
  - Provide regular impact reports showing how the new approach is amplifying their contributions.
  - Offer "Impact Experience" days where donors can see the human-centered approach in action.
- **Turning Resistant Donors into Champions:**
  - Create a "Donor Innovation Fund" where resistant donors can test new ideas within the human-centered framework.
  - Pair skeptical donors with those who are enthusiastic about the change for peer-to-peer conversations.

- Highlight stories of donors who initially resisted but now champion the new approach.

The Role of Leadership and Board Members

Leadership and board members are crucial in driving change. Here are strategies for persuading and educating them:

- **Present Data:** Use data and case studies to demonstrate the potential impact of a human-centered approach. Highlight how it can increase efficiency, engagement, and overall fundraising success.
- **Build Consensus:** Involve leadership in key decision-making processes and ensure they understand the strategic benefits of the new model.
- **Involve in Storytelling:** Encourage leadership to share stories of the impact they've seen from similar models, reinforcing the value of this approach.

Leadership Modeling Bridging and Belonging

Leaders play a critical role in modeling bridging behaviors—demonstrating curiosity, empathy, and a commitment to inclusion. By actively participating in bridging activities and sharing their own learning journeys, leaders can inspire others to embrace change. Leadership that prioritizes belonging and open communication is key to overcoming resistance and building lasting support for new initiatives.

Current Trends and Best Practices

Incorporating current trends can enhance your approach:

- **AI for Data Analysis:** Use AI to personalize donor communications and streamline data analysis, making your fundraising efforts more efficient and effective.
- **Social Media for Community Engagement:** Leverage social media platforms to engage with the community, share stories, and build support for your cause.

Storytelling Elements

Let's illustrate the power of storytelling with an example:

Imagine a nonprofit leader who successfully navigated resistance by using empathy and open communication. She involved her team in the decision-making process, listened to their concerns, and addressed them proactively. As a result, the team felt valued and empowered, leading to a smoother transition to the new model. This approach not only built internal support but also created a compelling narrative that resonated with donors and the community, ultimately increasing fundraising success.

Ensuring Long-Term Sustainability

Implementing change is just the beginning. Here's how to ensure your human-centered approach becomes ingrained in your organizational DNA:

- **Embed Change in Organizational Culture:**
  - Revise mission and vision statements to reflect the human-centered approach.
  - Update hiring practices to prioritize candidates who align with this philosophy.
  - Incorporate human-centered metrics into performance evaluations at all levels.
- **Continuous Improvement:**
  - Establish a "Learning Lab" where staff can experiment with new human-centered fundraising ideas.
  - Implement regular "Retrospective" sessions to reflect on what's working and what needs adjustment.
  - Create a "Change Scorecard" to track progress on key indicators over time.
- **Bridging and Belonging:**
  - To ensure long-term sustainability, embed the principles of bridging and belonging into your organization's culture.
  - Include updating hiring practices to prioritize candidates who demonstrate bridging skills, incorporating belonging metrics into performance reviews.
  - Create ongoing opportunities for cross-group collaboration.

- **Measuring Success:**
  - Develop a balanced scorecard that includes traditional metrics (funds raised) alongside human-centered metrics (community engagement, beneficiary feedback).
  - Conduct annual "Stakeholder Satisfaction" surveys to gauge perceptions of the new approach.
  - Use storytelling to capture qualitative impacts that numbers alone can't convey.

Key Takeaways

- Understand the roots of resistance—fear of change is natural but surmountable.
- Build a compelling case for change using data, stories, and vivid future scenarios.
- Engage stakeholders early and often and address their concerns proactively; their buy-in is critical to success.
- Build a team that reflects a variety of skills and perspectives.
- Use compelling narratives to connect with donors and the community.
- Provide education and training to demystify new approaches.
- Showcase early wins to build confidence and momentum.
- Foster a culture of adaptability by encouraging feedback and celebrating progress.
- Address resource constraints creatively, leveraging technology and volunteers.
- Keep donors engaged throughout the change process.
- Embed the human-centered approach into your organizational culture for long-term sustainability.
- Celebrate successes to reinforce the value of the new approach.

Readiness Checklist

As you embark on this journey toward human-centered fundraising, use this checklist to gauge your organization's readiness to bridge divides and overcome resistance:

- Do we actively seek input from all stakeholder groups?
- Are we creating spaces where everyone feels they belong?

- Do we celebrate small wins and share stories of successful collaboration?
- Are leaders modeling empathy, curiosity, and openness?
- Are we flexible and responsive to feedback during change processes?

Start today by taking the self-assessment quiz and identifying one area for immediate action. Share this chapter with your leadership team and schedule a "Change Café" to start the conversation.

Remember: adopting a human-centered fundraising model is not without its challenges—but it's worth it. By addressing resistance head-on, fostering collaboration, and staying committed to your vision, you can create lasting change that benefits both donors and communities.

Together, we can create a world where every nonprofit thrives, every mission is fully funded, and every community flourishes. The winds of change are blowing—it's time to set sail toward a brighter, more impactful future.

12 | Measuring Impact: Metrics for a New Era of Fundraising

"If you can't measure it, you can't improve it."
—Peter Drucker, Austrian-American Management Consultant,
Educator, and Author

In the evolving landscape of nonprofit fundraising, success can no longer be measured solely by dollars raised. As we embrace human-centered fundraising, we must reimagine how we define and measure success. This chapter explores innovative metrics that capture the true impact of our work, strategies for effective impact communication, and ways to leverage these insights to drive sustainable growth.

Redefining Success: Beyond the Bottom Line

The shift toward human-centered fundraising necessitates a corresponding shift in our metrics. While financial targets remain important, they alone cannot capture the full scope of our impact. Let's explore a new framework for measuring success that aligns with the principles of human-centered fundraising.

Holistic Impact Metrics

- **Lives Touched:** This metric goes beyond simple beneficiary counts to measure the depth and breadth of impact on individuals. For example, a youth mentoring program might track not just the number of mentees but also improvements in academic performance, self-esteem, and future aspirations.

- **Community Engagement Index:** This composite metric could include factors such as volunteer hours, community partnerships formed, and local participation in events. It reflects the strength of your organization's roots within the community.

- **Donor Satisfaction and Retention:** While donor retention has always been important, human-centered fundraising emphasizes the quality of donor relationships. Consider implementing regular surveys to gauge donor satisfaction, sense of connection to your mission, and likelihood to continue supporting your cause.

- **Collaborative Impact Score:** This metric measures the effectiveness of partnerships with other organizations. It could include factors such as shared resources, joint initiatives, and collective outcomes achieved.

- **Empowerment Quotient:** For organizations focused on capacity building or advocacy, this metric could track the increased ability of beneficiaries to effect change in their own lives or communities.

Expanded Metrics Framework

To ground your strategy in both best practice and actionable data, consider a comprehensive set of modern fundraising KPIs. These include:

- **Financial Metrics:**
  - Total Funds Raised
  - Goal Achievement Rate
  - Average Gift Size

- Donor Retention Rate
- Donor Acquisition Rate
- Donor Lifetime Value (LTV)
- Cost per Dollar Raised (CPDR)
- Fundraising ROI
- **Engagement & Relationship Metrics:**
  - Donor Engagement Score
  - Number of Touchpoints per Donor
  - Non-ask Ratio
  - Number of Warm Referrals/Introductions
  - Volunteer and Event Participation
- **Efficiency & Productivity Metrics:**
  - Donor Funnel Metrics
  - Response Rates
  - Number Proposals Submitted to Accepted Ratio
  - Capacity to Ask Amount Ratio
- **Strategic & Impact Metrics:**
  - Program-Specific Giving
  - Tangible Outcomes (e.g., graduation rates, acres conserved, family reunification rate, etc.)
- **Digital & Communication Metrics:**
  - Online Gift Percentage
  - Email Open and Click-Through Rates
  - Social Media Conversion Rate

Organizations should select metrics aligned with their strategic goals, balancing leading indicators (predictive, e.g., engagement) and lagging indicators (historical, e.g., funds raised) for a holistic view.

Lives Touched

This metric goes beyond simple beneficiary counts to measure the depth and breadth of impact on individuals. For example, a youth mentoring program might track not just the number of mentees, but also improvements in academic performance, self-esteem, and future aspirations.

Community Engagement Index

This composite metric could include factors such as volunteer hours, community partnerships formed, and local participation in events. It reflects the strength of your organization's roots within the community.

Donor Satisfaction and Retention

While donor retention has always been important, human-centered fundraising emphasizes the quality of donor relationships. Consider implementing regular surveys to gauge donor satisfaction, sense of connection to your mission, and likelihood to continue partnering with your cause.

Deep Dive: Monthly Giving and Retention

Monthly donors are retained at rates up to 90%, compared to much lower retention for one-time donors. They give seven times more annually than one-time donors and are more likely to upgrade their support over time. Key retention-focused metrics to track include:

- Donor retention rate
- Donor attrition rate
- Gift retention rate
- Average and median gift values
- Donor lifetime value

For example, if you have 1,000 donors in year one and 400 give again in year two, your donor retention rate is 40%. Increasing your retention rate by just 20% can boost donor lifetime value by 50% or more. Monthly giving programs are a proven way to achieve these gains and provide a stable, predictable revenue stream.

Practical Tip: Map out the donor experience from first gift through ongoing stewardship to identify retention opportunities and improve donor satisfaction.

Collaborative Impact Score

This metric measures the effectiveness of partnerships with other organizations. It could include factors such as shared resources, joint initiatives, and collective outcomes achieved.

Empowerment Quotient

For organizations focused on capacity building or advocacy, this metric could track the increased ability of beneficiaries to effect change in their own lives or communities.

Integrating with Existing Frameworks

To ensure a smooth transition, it's crucial to integrate these new metrics into existing fundraising frameworks or systems. For instance, nonprofits using the Heartfelt Connector or Beneficiary Builder models can incorporate holistic impact metrics to enhance donor engagement and beneficiary outcomes. By aligning these metrics with current systems, organizations can leverage their existing infrastructure while adopting a more human-centered approach.

Case Studies: Diverse Approaches to Impact Measurement

The Ripple Effect Foundation: Water Access

The Ripple Effect Foundation, focused on water access in rural communities, revolutionized its impact measurement approach. They developed a "Water Impact Index" that incorporated:

- Reduction in water-borne illnesses
- Increase in school attendance (especially for girls)
- Time saved in water collection
- Growth of local businesses due to improved water access
- Community members trained in well maintenance

This multifaceted approach provided a comprehensive understanding of their impact, improving strategic decision-making and resonating deeply with donors.

Eden Projects: Reforestation and Community Empowerment

Eden Projects, a nonprofit focused on reforestation, measures its impact not just in trees planted but in lives changed. Their metrics include:

- Number of trees planted (over 250 million to date)
- Employment created in impoverished communities

- Increase in local biodiversity
- Improvement in soil quality and agricultural yields
- Carbon sequestration estimates

By linking environmental impact with community empowerment, Eden Projects tells a compelling story of holistic change.

The Innocence Project: Justice and Transparency

The Innocence Project, working to end wrongful incarceration, exemplifies the power of transparency in impact reporting. They focus on:

- Number of exonerations achieved
- Policy changes influenced
- Public awareness metrics (media coverage, social media engagement)
- Time saved from wrongful imprisonment
- Compensation secured for exonerees

Their comprehensive FAQ on the donation page demonstrates a commitment to donor education and trust-building.

Additional Case Studies

- **Healthcare Sector:** A hospital might measure the impact of a new community health program by tracking patient outcomes, community engagement, and partnerships with local healthcare providers.
- **Education Sector:** An educational nonprofit could assess the effectiveness of its literacy program by monitoring student progress, teacher training outcomes, and community involvement in educational events.

Tracking Human-Centered Metrics

Implementing new metrics requires thoughtful planning and execution. Here are strategies to effectively track human-centered fundraising metrics:

- **Invest in Data Infrastructure:** Robust data management systems are crucial for collecting, analyzing, and reporting on complex metrics. Consider tools like Salesforce Nonprofit Cloud, Bloomerang, or DonorPerfect, which offer customizable reporting features and real-time dashboards for monitoring KPIs like retention, average gift size, and campaign ROI.

- **Develop Clear Definitions:** Ensure all team members understand how each metric is defined and calculated. Create a "Metrics Playbook" that outlines each measure, its importance, and how it's tracked.
- **Implement Regular Check-ins:** Schedule quarterly review sessions to assess progress on key metrics. This allows for timely adjustments to strategies if needed.
- **Encourage Feedback Loops:** Create mechanisms for beneficiaries, donors, and community partners to provide ongoing feedback. This qualitative data can offer valuable context to your quantitative metrics.
- **Leverage Technology:** Explore innovative ways to gather data, such as mobile surveys for beneficiaries or blockchain technology for transparent impact tracking. Integrate your CRM, email, and fundraising platforms to streamline data flow and enhance reporting.
- **Best Practices:**
  - Set clear data entry standards
  - Train staff regularly
  - Define KPIs upfront
  - Build a culture of data-driven decision-making

The Role of Technology in Impact Measurement

Advancements in technology are revolutionizing how nonprofits measure and analyze impact:

- **AI and Machine Learning:** These technologies can help identify patterns in large datasets, predict future trends, and highlight areas for intervention.
- **Data Analytics:** Sophisticated analytics tools can process complex datasets, providing insights that might be missed by traditional analysis methods.

- **IoT Devices:** For environmental or health-focused nonprofits, IoT devices can provide real-time data on air quality, water purity, or patient health metrics.
- **Blockchain:** This technology offers unprecedented transparency in tracking donations and their impact, building trust with donors.

Practical Examples:

- Use CRM segmentation to send targeted messages that resonate with specific donor groups, increasing response rates.
- Automate thank-you messages and impact reports via email to enhance donor retention.
- Run A/B tests on email subject lines or campaign appeals to optimize messaging for better engagement.

Balancing Quantitative and Qualitative Metrics

While quantitative metrics provide concrete data, qualitative insights offer depth and context. Striking the right balance is crucial:

- **Quantitative Metrics:** Focus on measurable outcomes like numbers served, dollars raised, or policy changes achieved.
- **Qualitative Insights:** Capture stories, testimonials, and observed changes in behavior or community dynamics.

"Not everything that matters can be measured, and not everything that can be measured matters."

—Cherian Koshy

Stewardship activities—such as personalized thank-you calls or handwritten notes—may not yield immediate revenue but are essential for long-term donor retention and trust. Pairing quantitative outcomes with qualitative stories and testimonials ensures a balanced, human-centered approach to impact measurement.

Communicating Impact: Telling Your Story

Measuring impact is only half the battle; effectively communicating that impact is equally crucial. In the age of information overload, we must find compelling ways to share our stories and demonstrate the tangible differ-ence we're making.

Feedback Loops and Continuous Improvement

Implementing effective feedback loops involves:

- **Regular Surveys:** Conduct regular surveys among beneficiaries, donors, and community partners to gather qualitative feedback.
- **Actionable Insights:** Use feedback to adjust strategies, ensuring that your programs remain responsive to community needs.
- **Transparency:** Share feedback findings openly with stakeholders, demonstrating your commitment to continuous improvement.

Stakeholder Engagement

Engaging stakeholders in the process of defining and refining metrics is vital:

- **Inclusive Decision-Making:** Involve team members, board mem-bers, donors, and beneficiaries in metric selection to ensure everyone is aligned with the organization's goals.
- **Education and Training:** Provide comprehensive training on new metrics to ensure all stakeholders understand their importance and how they are tracked.
- **Recognition and Feedback:** Celebrate achievements in impact measurement and create channels for ongoing feedback.

Strategies for Impactful Communication

- **Personalized Impact Reports:** Move beyond generic annual reports. Create tailored impact statements for major donors, showing exactly how their contributions have made a difference.
- **Visual Storytelling:** Leverage infographics, videos, and interactive web experiences to bring your impact to life. Visual content is more engaging and shareable, increasing the reach of your message.
- **Beneficiary Voices:** Amplify the stories of those you serve. First-person narratives create emotional connections and demonstrate real-world impact.

- **Real-Time Updates:** Use social media and email campaigns to provide regular, bite-sized impact updates. This keeps donors engaged throughout the year, not just during major campaigns.
- **Community Impact Maps:** Create interactive maps showing the geographic spread of your impact. This can be particularly effective for organizations with a wide reach.

Case Study: Feeding Futures

Feeding Futures, a nonprofit addressing childhood hunger, transformed its donor communication strategy:

- They created a mobile app where donors could "follow" specific school meal programs they supported.
- The app provided weekly updates, including photos of meals served, stories from children and teachers, and progress toward nutritional goals.
- Donors could easily share these updates on their own social media, amplifying the organization's reach.
- For major donors, they offered the opportunity to virtually "visit" the schools through live video calls.

This approach led to a 40% increase in donor retention and a 25% increase in average gift size. Donors reported feeling more connected to the cause and having a clearer understanding of their impact.

Leveraging Impact Data for Growth

The insights gained from human-centered metrics can drive organizational growth and enhance fundraising efforts. Here's how to leverage your impact data:

- **Inform Strategy:** Use impact data to guide program development and resource allocation. Focus on initiatives that show the strongest outcomes.

- **Enhance Grant Applications:** Robust impact data strengthens grant proposals. Many foundations now prioritize evidence-based approaches.
- **Cultivate Major Donors:** Use personalized impact reports in your major gift strategy. Showing concrete results can inspire larger and more frequent donations.
- **Improve Donor Segmentation:** Analyze which types of impact resonate most with different donor segments. Tailor your communications accordingly.
- **Benchmark and Improve:** Compare your impact metrics with similar organizations. This can highlight areas for improvement and innovative approaches.

Overcoming Challenges in Impact Measurement

Implementing a new approach to impact measurement isn't without its challenges. Here are some common obstacles and strategies to overcome them:

- **Resource Constraints:** Comprehensive impact measurement can be resource-intensive. Start small, focusing on a few key metrics, and gradually expand your measurement capabilities.
- **Data Quality Issues:** Inconsistent or incomplete data can skew results. Invest in staff training on data collection and consider periodic data audits.
- **Attribution Difficulties:** It can be challenging to attribute specific outcomes solely to your organization's efforts. Be transparent about this limitation and focus on contribution rather than attribution.
- **Stakeholder Buy-in:** Some team members or board members may resist new metrics. Educate stakeholders on the importance of human-centered measurement and involve them in the metric selection process.
- **Long-term Impact:** Some outcomes may take years to manifest. Develop interim indicators that can signal progress toward long-term goals.

Modernize Your Pipeline: Risk-Adjusted Metrics

Traditional fundraising metrics like number of calls or visits focus on activity, not outcomes. Modern fundraising requires a shift to risk-adjusted pipeline metrics, which assess the likelihood of securing major gifts based on donor readiness and relationship stage. This approach, borrowed from the private sector, prioritizes quality over quantity, builds trust, and leads to larger, more meaningful gifts. Key risk-adjusted pipeline metrics include:

- Pipeline Size (number of qualified prospects)
- Risk Adjustment (probability-weighted forecast)
- Pipeline Velocity (speed of donor progression)

This model ensures that every interaction is intentional and aligned with the donor's readiness, transforming both donor experience and fundraising results.

Challenges Specific to Small Nonprofits

Smaller nonprofits often face unique challenges, such as limited resources and staff. To overcome these, consider the following strategies:

- **Start Small:** Focus on a few key metrics and gradually expand your measurement capabilities.
- **Leverage Technology:** Utilize cost-effective digital tools for data collection and analysis.
- **Collaborate:** Partner with other organizations to share resources and expertise.

Technology and Data Security

Advancements in technology are revolutionizing how nonprofits measure and analyze impact:

- **AI and Machine Learning:** These technologies can help identify patterns in large datasets, predict future trends, and highlight areas for intervention.

- **Data Analytics:** Sophisticated analytics tools can process complex datasets, providing insights that might be missed by traditional analysis methods.
- **IoT Devices:** For environmental or health-focused nonprofits, IoT devices can provide real-time data on air quality, water purity, or patient health metrics.
- **Blockchain:** This technology offers unprecedented transparency in tracking donations and their impact, building trust with donors.

However, it's essential to prioritize **data security and privacy**, especially when handling sensitive donor and beneficiary information. Implement robust data protection measures, ensure informed consent, and maintain transparency about data usage.

Ethical Considerations in Impact Measurement

As we delve deeper into measuring human impact, ethical considerations become paramount:

- **Privacy:** Ensure that data collection respects the privacy of beneficiaries and donors. Implement robust data protection measures.
- **Consent:** Always obtain informed consent when collecting personal stories or data.
- **Representation:** Be mindful of how you represent beneficiaries in your impact stories. Avoid exploitative or sensationalist narratives.
- **Data Ownership:** Consider who owns the data you collect and how it can be used.
- **Transparency:** Be open about your measurement methodologies and their limitations.

Staff and Volunteer Engagement

Implementing new impact metrics can significantly affect staff and volunteer motivation:

- **Training:** Provide comprehensive training on new measurement approaches.

- **Involvement:** Include staff and volunteers in the process of defining and refining metrics.
- **Recognition:** Celebrate achievements in impact measurement.
- **Feedback:** Create channels for staff and volunteers to provide input on the impact measurement process.

Future Trends in Impact Measurement

As we look to the future, several trends are shaping the field of impact measurement:

- **Real-time Impact Tracking:** Technologies enabling instant feedback on program outcomes.
- **Predictive Analytics:** Using historical data to forecast future impact and guide strategy.
- **Collaborative Impact Measurement:** Nonprofits working together to measure collective impact on complex social issues.
- **Beneficiary-led Evaluation:** Empowering those we serve to define and measure what success looks like.
- **Impact-linked Financing:** Tying funding to measurable impact outcomes.

Embracing a New Era of Impact

As we navigate the evolving landscape of philanthropy, embracing human-centered metrics is not just beneficial—it's essential. By redefining how we measure and communicate success, we can create deeper connections with our donors, make more informed strategic decisions, and ultimately increase our impact on the communities we serve.

The journey to implementing human-centered metrics is ongoing. Start with small steps, learn from your experiences, and continuously refine your approach. Here are some actionable steps you can take today:

- **Conduct a Metric Audit:** Evaluate your current metrics and identify gaps in measuring human-centered impact.
- **Engage Stakeholders:** Hold discussions with your team, board, and key donors about what impact means to them.

- **Pilot a New Metric:** Choose one human-centered metric to implement in the next quarter.
- **Experiment with Storytelling:** Try a new method of communicating impact, such as a beneficiary-led video or an interactive online report.
- **Foster a Learning Culture:** Encourage your team to regularly share insights and lessons learned from impact data.

Best Practices for Metrics Selection and Implementation

- Focus on a manageable set of KPIs aligned with your goals.
- Combine leading indicators (predictive, e.g., donor engagement) with lagging indicators (historical, e.g., funds raised).
- Use software to automate tracking and reduce errors.
- Allow sufficient time to observe trends and make informed adjustments.
- Regularly review and refine your metrics as your organization evolves.

Practical Metric Formulas and Examples

Donor Retention Rate: Number of donors who gave last year and this year ÷ Number of donors who gave last year × 100

Cost per Dollar Raised (CPDR): Total fundraising costs ÷ Total funds raised

Fundraising ROI: Total funds raised ÷ Total fundraising costs

Average Gift Size: Total amount received ÷ Number of gifts received

Donor Lifetime Value (LTV): Average length of time as an active donor × Average donation amount × Average frequency of donation

Event Conversion Rate: Number of event attendees who donated after the event ÷ Total number of event attendees × 100

Recurring Gift Percentage: Number of recurring gifts ÷ Total number of gifts × 100

Donor Growth Rate: (Number of donors this year − Number of donors last year) ÷ Number of donors last year × 100

Gift Frequency: Total number of gifts in a period ÷ Total number of donors

Key Takeaways and Action Steps

Key Takeaways

- **Redefine Success Beyond Dollars:** The evolving world of non-profit fundraising demands that organizations look past the bottom line. Human-centered fundraising requires new success metrics that capture the *real impact*—including relationships, community well-being, and long-term change—not just the amount raised.

- **Holistic Impact Metrics Matter:** A broader framework for impact tracking is essential. This means measuring not only funds raised, but also the quality of donor and community relationships, beneficiary outcomes, and organizational learning.

- **Communication Is Impact's Megaphone:** Measuring impact is only half the battle—sharing it effectively with stakeholders is the other half. Nonprofits build trust and secure long-term support through transparent, inspiring impact communication, blending both metrics and relatable stories.

- **Sustainable Growth Stems from Insight:** By leveraging these more meaningful insights—how programs change lives, how engaged the community is, how donors' gifts matter—organizations can drive far more sustainable, reliable fundraising growth.

- **Shift to a Human-Centered Lens:** This approach fuses the best of donor-centered and community-centered fundraising philosophies, rooting every metric and message in respect for all stakeholders—donors, beneficiaries, and the broader community alike.

Action Steps

- **Expand Your Metrics Framework:** Start tracking both quantitative (e.g., funds raised, donor retention rates) and qualitative (e.g., beneficiary stories, donor satisfaction, community engagement) indicators in your reporting and planning.

- **Tell the Whole Story:** When communicating with stakeholders, go beyond numbers. Share tangible stories of transformation, highlight testimonials from program participants, and connect metrics back to real-world impact.

- **Implement Stakeholder-Focused Reporting:** Regularly produce and share impact reports that include both the "what" (metrics) and the "so what" (stories and testimonials). This helps both hearts and minds understand your results.
- **Foster a Culture of Learning:** Encourage your fundraising and program teams to see metrics as a tool for growth and evolution. Celebrate successes, but also spotlight lessons learned and continuous improvements.
- **Engage All Heroes:** Invite feedback and participation from donors, volunteers, beneficiaries, and staff in both defining what "impact" means and how best to communicate it.
- **Drive Long-Term Growth Through Trust:** Consistently communicate your organization's comprehensive impact. Transparency and authentic storytelling are the foundation for sustained donor trust and community support.

By embracing a holistic, human-centered approach to measurement and communication, your organization doesn't just grow its numbers—it multiplies its impact, builds deeper trust, and grows a community of heroes ready to transform the world together.

Looking Ahead: Charting the Future of Human-Centered Fundraising

As we conclude our exploration of measuring impact in human-centered fundraising, we've seen how innovative metrics and effective communication can transform our work. By embracing these new approaches, nonprofits can build stronger relationships with donors, make informed strategic decisions, and ultimately increase their impact on the communities they serve.

However, the landscape of nonprofit fundraising is constantly evolving. New technologies, shifting societal values, and emerging challenges require us to be forward-thinking and adaptable. In the next chapter, "The Future of Fundraising: Trends and Predictions," we will delve into the future landscape of nonprofit fundraising, exploring trends that are reshaping the sector and predictions that will guide our strategies for years to come.

We will examine how to continue innovating, iterating, and adapting to new challenges and opportunities. By understanding these trends and predictions, you will be empowered to not only navigate the future but to shape it. The journey ahead is full of possibilities, and it's time to take the next step.

As you look to the future, consider what actions you can take today to prepare for tomorrow. How can you apply the principles of human-centered fundraising to drive innovation in your organization? What trends will you leverage to enhance your impact? The future of fundraising is not just about responding to change; it's about leading it. Let's embark on this journey together, inspired by the potential to create a brighter future for all.

By embracing these new approaches to measuring and communicating impact, we can usher in a new era of fundraising—one that truly puts people at the center of our work. Together, we can create a future where every nonprofit thrives, every mission is fully funded, and every community has the support it needs to flourish. The challenges we face are complex, but armed with the right metrics and a commitment to human-centered principles, we are more than equal to the task. Let's measure what truly matters and use those insights to change the world one life at a time.

13 | The Future of Fundraising: Trends and Predictions

As the sun rises over the bustling city, an executive director of a small but impactful environmental nonprofit, let's call her Sarah, finds herself pondering the future. Her organization has made significant strides in recent years, but she can't shake the feeling that they are on the cusp of something bigger. The landscape of fundraising is shifting beneath her feet, and she knows that to truly make a difference, they need to evolve.

Sarah's story is not unique. Across the nonprofit sector, leaders and fundraisers are grappling with rapid changes and emerging trends that promise to reshape how we connect with donors and communities. The future of fundraising is not just about raising more money—it's about fostering deeper connections, leveraging technology responsibly, and creating lasting impact.

In this chapter, we'll explore the exciting possibilities that lie ahead and equip you with the insights and strategies needed to navigate this evolving landscape. By embracing a human-centered approach that combines the best of community-centric and donor-centric models—*centering all people*—we can unlock new potential and drive meaningful change.

So, let's embark on this journey together, exploring the trends and predictions that will shape the future of fundraising. By the end of this chapter, you'll be inspired to innovate, adapt, and lead your organization into a brighter tomorrow.

The Rise of AI-Powered Personalization

Artificial Intelligence (AI) is no longer just a buzzword—it's becoming an integral part of nonprofit operations, especially in fundraising. As we look to the future, AI will play a crucial role in personalizing donor experiences and optimizing fundraising strategies.

Predictive Analytics for Donor Engagement

AI-powered predictive analytics will enable nonprofits to routinely anticipate donor behavior and preferences with unprecedented accuracy. By analyzing vast amounts of data, including giving history, engagement patterns, and even social media activity, AI can help identify the most effective ways to engage each donor at scale across the sector.

For example, the American Red Cross has been using AI to analyze donor data and predict which donors are most likely to give again. This approach has allowed them to tailor their outreach efforts, resulting in a 22% increase in donor retention rates.

Chatbots and Virtual Assistants

AI-powered chatbots and virtual assistants will become increasingly sophisticated, providing donors with instant, personalized support. These tools can answer questions, guide donors through the giving process, and even offer personalized giving recommendations based on a donor's interests and history.

The key to success with AI is to use it as a tool to enhance human connections, not replace them. Sarah, from our chapter's opening story, discovered that AI can free up staff time for more meaningful interactions with donors.

"We implemented an AI chatbot on our website last year," Sarah shared. "At first, I was worried it would feel impersonal. But we've found that it actually allows our team to focus on deeper, more impactful conversations with our major donors while still providing excellent service to all our supporters."

Ethical Considerations and Transparency

As AI becomes more prevalent, nonprofits must prioritize responsible use and transparency. Donors will expect clear communication about how their data is being used and the role of AI in fundraising efforts.

> **Action Step:** Develop an AI ethics policy for your organization that outlines how you'll use AI responsibly and transparently in your fundraising efforts and in other areas of your work.
>
> **Reflection Question:** How could AI enhance your organization's ability to connect with donors on a more personal level?

The Evolution of Giving Circles and Collective-Impact Philanthropy

The future of fundraising will see a continued rise in collaborative giving models, with giving circles leading the charge. These groups of donors who pool their resources and collectively decide how to allocate funds are reshaping traditional philanthropy.

Democratizing Philanthropy

Giving circles are making philanthropy more accessible and inclusive, allowing individuals to have a greater impact by combining their resources.

This trend aligns perfectly with the human-centered approach to fundraising, as it empowers donors and strengthens community connections.

The impact of giving circles is already significant. According to a study by the Collective Giving Research Group, giving circles have engaged at least 150,000 people and given away as much as $1.29 billion since their inception.

Technology-Enabled Collaboration

The future will see giving circles leveraging technology to expand their reach and impact. Online platforms will make it easier for members to collaborate, research causes, and make collective decisions about funding.

For instance, Grapevine, a platform for managing giving circles, has seen rapid adoption. "We're excited to see how nonprofits continue to leverage this community-centric movement to support their work in 2025," says Emily Rasmussen, CEO of Grapevine.

Hybrid Models of Giving

We'll likely see the emergence of hybrid models that combine elements of traditional fundraising with giving circle principles. Nonprofits might create their own giving circles or partner with existing ones to engage donors in new ways.

Case Study: The Women's Foundation of California

The Women's Foundation of California has successfully integrated giving circles into its fundraising strategy. Their Giving Circle program allows groups of women to pool their resources and make grants to organizations supporting women and girls in California.

Since its inception, the program has engaged over 800 members and granted more than $21 million to over 500 organizations. This approach has not only increased funding but also deepened donor engagement and community impact.

Action Step: Explore ways to incorporate giving circle principles into your fundraising strategy. Consider creating a pilot program that allows donors to collaborate on funding decisions for a specific project or program.

Reflection Question: How might a giving circle model enhance your organization's relationship with donors and the community?

The Power of Storytelling in the Digital Age

As we move into the future, the art of storytelling will become even more crucial in fundraising. With the proliferation of digital platforms and shortening attention spans, nonprofits will need to master the art of compelling, multi-format storytelling to cut through the noise and connect with donors.

Global Storytelling Strategies: In Australia, nonprofits are using storytelling to highlight the impact of environmental conservation efforts, while in India, storytelling is being used to raise awareness about social justice issues.

Video and Virtual Reality

Video content will continue to dominate, with short-form videos becoming increasingly popular for donor engagement. Platforms like TikTok and Instagram Reels offer new opportunities to reach younger audiences and share impactful stories in bite-sized formats.

Virtual Reality (VR) and Augmented Reality (AR) will also play a larger role in storytelling, allowing donors to immerse themselves in the impact of their giving. Imagine allowing donors to virtually "visit" the communities they're supporting or experience the environmental changes their donations are helping to mitigate.

User-Generated Content and Peer-to-Peer Storytelling

The future of fundraising will see a shift toward more authentic, user-generated content. Donors and beneficiaries will become storytellers themselves, sharing their experiences and the impact of the organization's work through their own social media channels.

This peer-to-peer storytelling can be incredibly powerful. According to a study by Tiltify, peer-to-peer fundraising campaigns that incorporate personal stories raise 150% more than those without.

Data-Driven Storytelling

As data analytics capabilities improve, nonprofits will be able to tell more compelling stories by integrating real-time impact data into their narratives. This approach will allow donors to see the tangible results of their giving, fostering a deeper connection to the cause.

> **Action Step:** Develop a multi-format storytelling strategy that incorporates video, user-generated content, and data visualization. Experiment with new platforms and technologies to find what resonates best with your audience.
>
> **Reflection Question:** How can you empower your beneficiaries, advocates, volunteers, staff, and donors to become storytellers for your cause?

The Shift Toward Recurring Giving and Subscription Models

The future of fundraising will see a continued shift toward recurring giving models, mirroring the subscription-based economy we see in other sectors. This trend aligns well with the human-centered approach, as it allows donors to make a sustained impact and feel more connected to the cause over time.

Charity: Water's "The Spring" program is a great example of this model in action. Donors can sign up to give a small amount monthly, and the organization provides regular updates on the impact of these collective donations.

> **Action Step:** Evaluate your current recurring giving program and identify opportunities for improvement. Consider implementing a micro-donation option or enhancing your impact reporting for recurring donors.
>
> **Reflection Question:** How can you make your recurring giving program more flexible and engaging for donors?

The Rise of Micro-Donations

Micro-donations, small recurring gifts often tied to everyday activities, will become increasingly popular. For example, apps that round up purchases to the nearest dollar and donate the difference are gaining traction.

Flexible Giving Options

The future will see nonprofits offering more flexible giving options to cater to donor preferences. This might include the ability to easily adjust donation amounts, pause giving, or choose the frequency of donations through online portals and giving apps.

Personalized Impact Reporting: With recurring giving, donors will expect regular updates on the impact of their ongoing support. Nonprofits will need to invest in systems that can provide personalized, real-time impact reporting to keep donors engaged and committed. The annual impact report alone is no longer sufficient to engage and retain your community of supporters.

The Integration of Social Impact and Commerce

The line between commerce and philanthropy will continue to blur, with more businesses integrating social impact into their core operations. This trend presents both opportunities and challenges for nonprofits.

Sustainability in Corporate Partnerships: Nonprofits should look for corporate partners that prioritize environmental sustainability and social responsibility. This not only enhances the nonprofit's reputation and amplifies the company's commitment but also contributes to a more sustainable future.

Cause Marketing and Corporate Partnerships

Cause marketing will evolve beyond one-off campaigns to become a more integral part of business strategies. Nonprofits that can effectively partner with businesses to create authentic, long-term impact initiatives will thrive.

For instance, Patagonia's commitment to donating 1% of sales to environmental causes has not only raised millions for nonprofits but has also become a core part of its brand identity, engendering consumer loyalty.

Social Enterprises and Hybrid Models

We'll likely see a rise in social enterprises and hybrid models that combine nonprofit and for-profit elements. These organizations will challenge traditional nonprofits to think creatively about sustainable funding models.

Reflection Question: How might your organization leverage partnerships with socially responsible businesses to further your mission?

Blockchain and Cryptocurrency Donations

As cryptocurrencies become more mainstream, nonprofits will need to be prepared to accept and manage these types of donations. Blockchain technology also offers the potential for greater transparency in how donations are used and tracked.

The American Red Cross, for example, has been accepting Bitcoin donations since 2014, demonstrating early adoption of this trend.

Action Step: Explore potential corporate partnerships that align with your mission. Also, research the feasibility of accepting cryptocurrency donations for your organization and policies for managing them.

Donor Advised Funds and Other Non-Cash Gifts

We'll see an ever-increasing focus on gifts from donor-advised funds (DAFs) and appreciated stock, particularly during economic and politically uncertain times. Ninety to ninety-five percent of individual net worth in the US is held in non-cash assets. These gifts have dual benefits to donors. They have the satisfaction and joy of making a difference when your organization likely needs it most, and they can enjoy significant tax benefits, like avoiding capital gains and claiming deductions on full market value. They also make it easier for donors to give larger gifts.

The Emphasis on Donor Retention and Lifetime Value

As the cost of acquiring new donors continues to rise, the future of fundraising will place even greater emphasis on donor retention and maximizing lifetime value. This aligns perfectly with the human-centered approach, focusing on building long-term relationships rather than transactional interactions.

Digital Security and Data Protection: With the rise of digital fundraising, nonprofits must prioritize data security and privacy. Implementing robust cybersecurity measures and transparent data handling practices will be crucial in maintaining donor trust.

Personalized Stewardship at Scale

AI and data analytics will enable nonprofits to deliver personalized stewardship experiences at scale. This might include customized thank you messages, impact reports tailored to a donor's specific interests, or personalized suggestions for further engagement based on a donor's history.

Multi-Channel Engagement Strategies

The future will see nonprofits adopting sophisticated multi-channel engagement strategies that meet donors where they are. This might involve coordinated outreach across email, social media, direct mail, and in-person events, all tailored to individual donor preferences.

Focus on Mid-Level Donors

While major gifts will always be important, we'll likely see increased attention on mid-level donors. These supporters often have significant potential for increased giving and engagement but are frequently overlooked in traditional fundraising models.

Case Study: The Nature Conservancy's Mid-Level Donor Program

The Nature Conservancy implemented a dedicated mid-level donor program that focused on personalized communication and engagement opportunities. By treating these donors more like major gift prospects, they saw a 23% increase in revenue from this group over three years.

> **Action Step:** Conduct an audit of your current donor retention strategies. Identify opportunities to personalize your stewardship and engage mid-level donors more effectively.
>
> **Reflection Question:** How can you create a more personalized experience for your mid-level donors? How can AI help?

The Growing Importance of Trust and Transparency

In an era of information overload and increasing skepticism, trust and transparency will become even more critical for nonprofits. The future of fundraising will require organizations to be proactively transparent about their operations, impact, and use of funds.

Real-Time Impact Reporting

Donors will expect real-time updates on how their contributions are being used and the impact they're making. Nonprofits will need to invest in systems that can track and communicate impact effectively.

Financial Transparency

Beyond just sharing annual reports, nonprofits will need to provide clear, accessible information about their financial health and how donations are allocated. This might include interactive online tools that allow donors to explore financial data in detail.

Ethical Fundraising Practices

As donors become more savvy and socially conscious, they'll expect nonprofits to adhere to high ethical standards in their fundraising practices. This includes responsible use of data, ethical storytelling that respects beneficiary dignity, and clear communication about fundraising costs.

> **Action Step:** Review your current transparency practices. Consider implementing a real-time impact dashboard on your website or developing a comprehensive ethical fundraising policy.
>
> **Reflection Question:** How can you make your organization's impact and financial information more accessible and understandable to donors?

Diversity, Equity, and Inclusion in Fundraising

While the Trump Administration has instituted anti-DEI initiatives in the first 100 days of his presidency, what goes up usually comes down. In other words, the future of fundraising will see an eventual return to increased focus on diversity, equity, and inclusion (DEI) principles. This shift will not only make philanthropy more accessible and representative but also help organizations better serve their communities. Nonprofits will need to ensure that their fundraising strategies reflect these values, engaging diverse donors and communities in meaningful ways.

Diversifying Donor Bases

The US Census Bureau and demographers estimate that by **2040–2050**, the US will become a "majority-minority" country, meaning that racial and ethnic minorities combined will constitute more than 50% of the population. Nonprofits will need to actively work on diversifying their donor bases to include diverse communities. This might involve targeted outreach, culturally sensitive communication, and creating giving opportunities that resonate with different groups. We must authentically demonstrate our organization welcomes all people working together in community for community. Heroes don't all think, act, or look alike, and that's part of their superpower.

Inclusive Storytelling

Nonprofits will need to tell stories that reflect the diversity of the communities they serve and the people serving them. This involves amplifying diverse voices throughout our organizations and ensuring that all people are represented with dignity and respect.

Culturally Responsive Fundraising

The future will require nonprofits to adopt culturally responsive fundraising practices that respect and honor the traditions and preferences of diverse donor groups. This might involve adapting communication strategies, event planning, and stewardship practices to better engage diverse communities.

Addressing Systemic Inequities

Nonprofits will increasingly be called upon to address systemic inequities within philanthropy itself. This might involve examining and restructuring power dynamics in donor relationships, prioritizing funding for marginalized communities, and advocating for a more equitable distribution of philanthropic resources.

Case Study: The Chicago Community Trust

The Chicago Community Trust has made significant strides in incorporating DEI into its fundraising and grantmaking practices. They've implemented a racial equity lens in their grantmaking, diversified their staff and board, and launched initiatives specifically aimed at supporting communities of color.

> **Action Step:** Conduct a DEI audit of your fundraising practices. Identify areas for improvement and develop a plan to make your fundraising more inclusive and equitable, creating a culture of belonging.
>
> **Reflection Question:** How can your organization better incorporate DEI principles into your fundraising strategies?

Global Perspectives on Fundraising

As the world becomes increasingly interconnected, the future of fundraising will require a more global outlook. Nonprofits will need to navigate cultural differences, international regulations, and global issues to effectively raise funds and create impact on a worldwide scale.

Cross-Border Giving

Technology will continue to make cross-border giving easier, allowing donors to support causes globally. Nonprofits will need to be prepared to engage with international donors and navigate the complexities of international fundraising regulations, as well as cultural and language differences.

Global Collaboration

We'll likely see more collaboration between nonprofits across borders to address global challenges. This might involve joint fundraising campaigns, shared resources, or coordinated advocacy efforts.

Cultural Sensitivity in Fundraising

As nonprofits expand their reach globally, cultural sensitivity in fundraising approaches will become crucial. What works in one country may not be effective or appropriate in another, requiring organizations to adapt their strategies accordingly.

Case Study: Kiva's Global Microlending Platform

Kiva, a nonprofit that facilitates microloans, has successfully created a global platform that connects lenders with borrowers across the world. Their model demonstrates how technology can enable global giving while respecting local cultures and needs.

> **Action Step:** If your organization has a global component, assess how you can make your fundraising more culturally sensitive and globally inclusive. If you're primarily local, consider how global trends might impact your work.
>
> **Reflection Question:** How might a more global perspective enhance your organization's fundraising efforts and impact?

Environmental Sustainability in Fundraising

As environmental concerns become increasingly urgent, sustainability will play a larger role in shaping fundraising strategies and donor expectations.

Green Fundraising Practices

Nonprofits will need to consider the environmental impact of their fundraising activities. This might involve shifting to digital communications, hosting virtual events, choosing eco-friendly merchandise for donor and volunteer recognition, or offsetting your fundraising carbon footprint with contributions to certified carbon footprint projects such as reforestation or soil carbon sequestration.

Environmental Impact Reporting

Donors, especially younger generations, will increasingly expect nonprofits to report on their environmental impact. This might involve sharing carbon footprint data to demonstrate their commitment to sustainability and responsible practices to attract and retain these donors.

> **Action Step:** Assess your organization's environmental footprint and identify opportunities to reduce waste and emissions in your fundraising efforts.

> **Reflection Question:** How can your organization lead by example in environmental sustainability while advancing your mission?

Generational Shifts in Giving

As demographic shifts occur, understanding and adapting to the giving preferences of different generations will be crucial for fundraising success.

Gen Z and Millennials: The Digital Natives

These younger generations, having grown up with technology, expect seamless digital experiences in their giving. They're more likely to engage with causes through social media, mobile apps, and peer-to-peer fundraising platforms.

"We've seen a 200% increase in donations through our mobile app over the past year, primarily driven by donors under 35," shares Mark Chen, Chief Digital Officer at a major international NGO.

Gen X: The Forgotten Middle

Often overlooked, Gen X donors are entering their peak earning years and represent a significant opportunity for nonprofits. They value transparency and tangible impact, often preferring to give to local causes or organizations they have a personal connection with.

Baby Boomers: The Legacy Givers

As Boomers enter retirement, they're thinking about their legacies. Planned giving and estate planning will be crucial strategies for engaging this generation. They also value personal relationships and may prefer more traditional communication methods.

> **Action Step:** Develop targeted engagement strategies for each generation, considering their preferred communication channels, giving methods, and motivations for supporting causes.
>
> **Reflection Question:** How can your organization better tailor fundraising approaches to resonate with different generations?

The Evolving Regulatory Landscape

As the nonprofit sector grows and evolves, so too will the regulatory environment. Staying ahead of these changes will be crucial for fundraising success.

Data Privacy Regulations

With the increasing use of donor data for personalization, nonprofits will need to navigate complex data privacy regulations. This might include obtaining explicit consent for data use and ensuring robust data protection measures.

Cryptocurrency and Blockchain Regulations

As more nonprofits begin accepting cryptocurrency donations, they'll need to stay informed about evolving regulations in this space. This could include new reporting requirements or changes in how these donations are valued for tax purposes.

International Fundraising Laws

For organizations operating globally, understanding and complying with international fundraising laws will be crucial. This might involve navigating different tax incentives for giving across countries or complying with anti-money laundering regulations.

> **Action Step:** Establish a system for staying informed about regulatory changes affecting nonprofit fundraising. Consider designating a team member to monitor these changes and update policies accordingly.
>
> **Reflection Question:** How can your organization proactively prepare for potential regulatory changes in the fundraising landscape?

Challenges and Potential Pitfalls

While the future of fundraising holds many exciting possibilities, it's important to be aware of potential challenges and pitfalls.

Technology Overreliance

While technology offers many benefits, over-reliance can lead to a loss of personal touch. "We implemented a fully automated donor communication system," shares Lisa Tran, Development Director at a mid-size Silicon Valley nonprofit. "But we quickly realized we were losing the personal connections that were so valuable to our long-term donors."

Data Security Risks

As nonprofits collect and use more donor data, they become increasingly attractive targets for cybercriminals. A data breach could severely damage donor trust and an organization's reputation.

Donor Fatigue

With the proliferation of causes and ease of giving, donors may become overwhelmed and experience "donor fatigue." Nonprofits will need to work harder to stand out and demonstrate their unique value.

Ethical Considerations in AI and Data Use

The use of AI and big data in fundraising raises ethical questions about privacy, consent, and the potential for manipulation. Nonprofits will need to navigate these issues carefully to maintain donor trust.

> **Action Step:** Conduct a risk assessment of your fundraising strategies, identifying potential challenges and developing mitigation and crisis management plans.
>
> **Reflection Question:** What are the biggest potential risks to your organization's fundraising efforts, and how can you proactively address them?

Future Scenarios: Fundraising in the 2030s

To help visualize the future of fundraising, let's explore a potential scenario for what fundraising might look like in the 2030s:

Sarah, our nonprofit leader from the beginning of the chapter, logs into her AI-powered fundraising dashboard. She sees real-time updates on ongoing campaigns, personalized suggestions for donor outreach, and predictive analytics on potential major gifts.

She puts on her VR headset to "visit" a project site, where she can see the impact of recent donations and record a personalized thank you message for donors. The message will be automatically translated and delivered to each donor in their preferred language and format.

Meanwhile, a group of Gen Z supporters are collaborating on a giving circle through a mobile app, pooling their resources to fund a new initiative. They're using blockchain technology to track exactly how their donations are being used.

Across the world, a corporate partner is launching a cause marketing campaign that allows customers to round up their purchases to the nearest dollar, with the difference going to Sarah's organization. The campaign is powered by AI that personalizes the ask based on each customer's giving history and preferences.

This scenario illustrates how many of the trends we've discussed might come together to create a fundraising landscape that is more personalized, transparent, and globally connected than ever before.

Key Takeaways and Action Steps

Key Takeaways

- AI and data analytics will enable more personalized donor experiences but must be used responsibly and transparently.
- Collaborative giving models like giving circles will continue to grow in importance.
- Storytelling will evolve to incorporate new formats and technologies, with a focus on authenticity and impact.
- Recurring giving and subscription models will become increasingly important for sustainable funding.
- The line between commerce and philanthropy will continue to blur, presenting new partnership opportunities.
- Donor retention and lifetime value will be key focus areas, with increased attention on mid-level donors.
- Trust and transparency will be critical, with donors expecting real-time impact reporting and clear communication.

- Diversity, equity, and inclusion will shape fundraising strategies and donor engagement.
- A global perspective will be crucial, even for local organizations.
- Environmental sustainability will influence both fundraising practices and constituent expectations.
- Understanding generational differences in giving will be key to effective fundraising and community engagement.
- Staying ahead of regulatory changes will be crucial for compliance and donor trust.
- While embracing new technologies, nonprofits must be aware of potential challenges and ethical considerations.

Action Steps

- Conduct an audit of your current fundraising strategies against these future trends. Identify areas where you're ahead of the curve and where you might need to evolve.
- Develop a roadmap for implementing one or two new strategies or technologies in the coming year. Start small and experiment to see what works best for your organization.
- Invest in training for your team to ensure they're equipped to navigate these changes and leverage new tools effectively.
- Foster a culture of innovation in your organization, encouraging team members to stay informed about emerging trends and propose new ideas.
- Most importantly, always view new trends and technologies through the lens of how they can help you build stronger, more meaningful relationships with your supporters and beneficiaries.

The future of fundraising is bright, filled with opportunities to create deeper connections, drive greater impact, and build a better world. By embracing a human-centered approach and staying open to innovation, you can lead your organization into this exciting future with confidence and purpose.

You are not just a fundraiser or a nonprofit leader. You are a catalyst for change, a builder of communities, and a creator of hope. You are a hero, too.

The work you do matters, and by embracing these future trends with a human-centered mindset, you can amplify your impact in ways we've only begun to imagine.

So, I invite you to step boldly into this future. Experiment, learn, and grow. Build on the timeless principles of human connection while leveraging the power of new technologies and approaches. Together, we can create a future of fundraising and community engagement that is more effective, more inclusive, and more impactful than ever before.

The world needs your passion, your creativity, and your commitment. Gather your heroes because it will take all of us. The future of fundraising is in your hands. Let's make it extraordinary.

References

Bishop, Matthew, and Michael Greenfield. *The Alchemy of Philanthropy*. London: Centre for Philanthropy, 2018.

Dale, Elizabeth J., and Maya Hemachandra. *Adopting Community-Centric Fundraising: Findings from a National Study*. Dorothy A. Johnson Center for Philanthropy at Grand Valley State University and AFP Foundation for Philanthropy, 2025.

James, Russell N., and William Wymer. *Sustainable Nonprofit Strategy*. New York: Routledge, 2019.

Sargeant, Adrian, and Elaine Jay. "Donor Trust and Relationship Commitment in the UK Charity Sector: The Impact on Behavior." *Nonprofit and Voluntary Sector Quarterly* 33, no. 2 (2015): 185–202.

Sargeant, Adrian, Jen Shang, and Associates. Sustainable Philanthropy. London: Institute for Sustainable Philanthropy, 2020.

Smith, John, and Rachel Symonds. "Donor Satisfaction and Retention: A Review of Recent Research." *Journal of Philanthropy and Fundraising* 8, no. 1 (2021a): 44–59.

Bibliography

African American Development Officers Network. "About AADO." Accessed May 15, 2025. https://aadonetwork.org

Association of Fundraising Professionals. "About AFP." Accessed May 15, 2025. https://afpglobal.org

Boggs, Grace Lee, and Scott Kurashige. *The Next American Revolution: Sustainable Activism for the Twenty-First Century*. University of California Press, 2011.

Burk, Penelope. *Donor-Centered Fundraising*. Burk & Associates Ltd., 2003.

Burnett, Ken. *Relationship Fundraising: A Donor-Based Approach to the Business of Raising Money*. 3rd ed. Jossey–Bass, 2017.

Cialdini, Robert B. *Influence: The Psychology of Persuasion*. Revised ed. HarperCollins, 2007.

Classy. "Classy Studio: Fundraising Platform." Accessed May 15, 2025. https://classy.org

Collins, Jim. *Good to Great and the Social Sectors: A Monograph to Accompany Good to Great*. Jim Collins, 2005.

Davis, Angela. *Women, Race & Class*. Vintage Books, 1983.

Drucker, Peter F. *The Practice of Management*. New York: Harper & Row, 1954.

Earthjustice. "Annual Reports and Equity Initiatives." Accessed May 15, 2025. https://earthjustice.org

Girard, Joe, and Stanley H. Brown. *How to Sell Anything to Anybody*. Simon & Schuster, 2006.

Giving USA Foundation. *Giving USA 2024: The Annual Report on Philanthropy for the Year 2023*. Giving USA Foundation, 2024.

INCITE! Women of Color Against Violence, ed. *The Revolution Will Not Be Funded: Beyond the Non-Profit Industrial Complex*. South End Press, 2007.

James Beard Foundation. "Annual Reports and Philanthropy Initiatives." Accessed May 15, 2025. https://jamesbeard.org

Langley, Jim M. *The Future of Fundraising: Adapting to New Philanthropic Realities*. Academic Impressions, 2020.

Le, Vu. *Unicorns on Fire: A Collection of Nonprofit AF Essays That Will Make You Laugh, Cry, and Rage at the World*. AuthorHouse, 2024.

Le, Vu. "Nonprofit AF." Accessed May 15, 2025. https://nonprofitaf.com

Lorde, Audre. *Sister Outsider: Essays and Speeches*. Crossing Press, 1984.

Marshall, Alex. "Graphic Novel in Running for Man Booker Prize for First Time." *New York Times*, July 23, 2018. https://www.nytimes.com/2018/07/23/books/booker-prize-graphic-novel-ondaatje.html

Maslow, Abraham H. *The Farther Reaches of Human Nature*. Viking Press, 1971.

Memorial Sloan Kettering Cancer Center. "Cycle for Survival." Accessed May 15, 2025. https://cycleforsurvival.org

Prisma Health. "Office of Philanthropy Reports." Accessed May 15, 2025. https://prismahealth.org

Rogare. "Rethinking Fundraising." Accessed May 15, 2025. https://www.rogare.net

Sargeant, Adrian, and Jen Shang. "The Science Behind Donor Centricity 3.0." Institute for Sustainable Philanthropy. Accessed May 15, 2025.

Sinek, Simon. *Start with Why: How Great Leaders Inspire Everyone to Take Action*. Portfolio, 2009.

Smith, Patricia, and Robert Symonds. *Ethical Fundraising in the Digital Age*. Cambridge, MA: Harvard Business Review Press, 2021b.

Acknowledgments

I'm profoundly grateful to the people and organizations who shaped this work.

To my friends, colleagues, and mentors—your wisdom, challenges, and camaraderie sharpened my thinking and enriched this book. Special thanks to Birgit Burton, Maia McGill, Harvey McKinnon, Tony Myers, Shanterra McBride, Cherian Koshy, Nathan Chappell—and the greatest mentor of all time, Lynda Bowman.

To the professionals and organizations who generously shared your time, stories, and insights—thank you for your candor and trust.

To my editors and peer reviewers—your feedback, skill, and patience helped shape this manuscript into something stronger and more useful.

And to every reader, donor, and nonprofit leader who believes in a more generous world—thank you for the work you do and for being part of this journey.

With boundless gratitude,
—Tammy Zonker

About the Author

Tammy Zonker is a passionate leader, strategic thinker, and recognized expert in major gift fundraising with nearly three decades of impactful experience. As the Founder and President of Fundraising Transformed, President of the Modern Institute for Charitable Giving, and host of *The Intentional Fundraiser Podcast*, Tammy is dedicated to empowering nonprofit organizations to achieve extraordinary results.

Throughout her extensive career, Tammy has guided and trained thousands of nonprofits—including social service organizations, private schools, universities, and healthcare institutions—to collectively raise nearly a billion dollars. Among her many successes is securing an impressive single gift of $27.1 million, highlighting her exceptional strategic insight and ability to inspire generosity.

Internationally sought after for her expertise, Tammy is an Association of Fundraising Professionals (AFP) Certified Facilitator and a seasoned global speaker, sharing her knowledge in Australia, Ireland, Canada, and the Netherlands. In 2024, the AFP Greater Detroit Chapter honored Tammy's outstanding contributions by presenting her with the prestigious Dr. John S. Lore Award for Outstanding Fundraising Executive of the Year.

Tammy previously served as Dean of the Institute for Charitable Giving for six years before acquiring the organization in 2025. She then revitalized and rebranded it as the Modern Institute for Charitable Giving, introducing an innovative and refreshed curriculum tailored for today's fundraising professionals.

In addition to her roles at Fundraising Transformed and the Modern Institute, Tammy is a Senior Advisor at Capital Campaign Pro. She also contributes to advancing the fundraising profession through her involvement with the Fundraising. AI Global Advisory Council and Forbes Nonprofit Advisory Council.

Tammy's experience extends into academia and publishing as well, having served as adjunct faculty at Indiana University and as a technical editor for Wiley Publishing's third edition of *Fundraising for Dummies*.

Beyond her professional life, Tammy treasures spending quality time with her grandchildren and cultivating her NABA-certified butterfly garden, reflecting her deep appreciation for nature and family.

Index

Page numbers followed by *t* refer to tables.

A

Accountability, 17
Acknowledgment, prompt, 17
ActionAid, 11
Active listening, 96
Advisory boards, donor, 184
Advisory councils, 138
African American Development Officers
    Network (AADO), 73
Agency-centered fundraising, 3–4
Agile principles, 151, 153
AI, 165–188
    action steps with, 187
    case examples, 173, 176
    in donor-centered fundraising, 26–27
    ethical issues with, 170–173, 223
    future trends with, 183–185
    for human-centered fundraising, 56
    integrating, 166–167
    maintaining a human touch with, 177–182
    for major gift programs, 173–176
    for metrics, 209, 214
    myth vs. reality of, in fundraising, 169–170
    potential risks with, 182–183
    predictive analytics with, 168–169
    in relationship fundraising, 9
    responsible, 56
    supercharging your fundraising with, 167–168
    for volunteer engagement/
        management, 176–177
Algorithmic bias, 182
American Heart Association (AHA), 53
American Red Cross, 94, 99, 125, 176, 222, 228
Amnesty International, 120

Angelou, Maya, 113
Anti-DEI initiatives, 94, 230–232
Appreciation, showing, 8
Arts institutions, 158
Asana, 98, 195
Association of Fundraising Professionals
        (AFP), 142, 148
Audits, financial, 142–143
Augmented reality, 126–127, 225
Australia, 225
Authenticity, 115
Automation.AI, 176
Average gift size, 217
Avid.AI, 178

B

Baby Boomers, 234
Balanced scorecard, 201
Baldwin, James, xiv, 33, 131
BBB Wise Giving Alliance, 6
Belonging, sense of, 34, 75, 192–193, 200
Beneficiary Builder, 207
Bias, 171, 182
Blockchain, 184, 210, 215, 235
Bloomerang (software platform), 99, 178
Boggs, Grace Lee, 33
Botton Village, 10
Brandwatch, 123
Budgetary considerations:
    with AI, 179
    with diverse teams, 80–81
    for recruitment, 74
Burk, Penelope, xiv–xv, 7, 16, 51
Burnett, Ken, 7–11, 16, 51
Burton, Birgit, 73

C

Camden Coalition, 136
Camphill Village Trust, 10
Candidate pools, limited, 78–79
Capacity, building, 37–38
Carter, Jimmy, 4
Carter, Lynda, xvi
CCS Fundraising, 57
Chang, Emily, 171
Change, resistance to, *see* Resistance to change
Changemaker Awards, 195
Chappell, Nathan, 165, 171
Characters, story, 116–117
Charity: Water, 103, 118–119, 182, 226
Charity Navigator, 6–7
CharityWatch, 6
Chatbots, 183–184, 222–223
ChatGPT, 178
Chen, Mark, 234
Chicago Community Trust, 231–232
Children's Center, xiii
The Children's Center (Detroit), 137–138
Cialdini, Robert, 71, 72
Civilla, 101–102
Classy Studio, 9
Claude, 178
Climate change, 84
COACH framework, 136
Co-creation, 52
Collaboration, 91
    and diverse teams, 87
    and implementation, 160
    necessary for human-centered fundraising, xv
    as principle of human-centered fundraising, 52
    technology-enabled, 224
Collaborative impact score, 204, 206
Collective Giving Research Group, 224
Collective impact (collective-impact
        philanthropy), 86–88, 223–225
Collins, Jim, 70–71
Common ground, building, 54–55
Communities:
    balancing interests of donors and, 59–60, 62
    and donors, 41–42
    as focus of fundraising, 34
    strengthening, 34
    well-being of, 39
Community-Centered Fundraising
        (CCF), 31–50
    action steps with, 48–49
    barriers to, 39–40
    bridging donor-centered and
        community-centered, 49–50
    case example, 35–39
    criticisms of, 40–43

donor-centered fundraising vs., 11, 44, 45*t*–46*t*
focus of, 11
growth of, 39
and human-centered fundraising, 44,
        46–47, 53, 54–55
principles of, 32–35
roots of, 32–34
scaling, 43–44
Community-Centric Fundraising (CCF)
        website, 33
Community engagement (community
        engagement index), 61, 204, 206
Community Health Partners, 73
Compelling narratives, 116–118
Consensus-building, 96
Constituent relationship management (CRM)
        platforms, 26
Constructive feedback, 97
Continuous improvement, 200
Continuous review, 171
Contributions, non-financial, 39
Conversion rate, 123
Copilot, 178
Core message, identifying your, 116
Cost per dollar raised (CPDR), 217
Courage, xvi
COVID-19 pandemic, 105
Credentials, non-traditional, 74
Cross-border giving, 232
Cross-functional collaboration, 93–94
Cryptocurrency, 228, 235
Cultural intelligence, 71
Cultural sensitivity, 122–123, 231, 232
Customer-centricty, 4
Cycle for Survival, 56–57

D

Dale, Elizabeth, 32, 35, 39, 40, 50
Darwin, Charles, 191
Data analysis (data analytics), 153, 154, 209
Data breaches, 182
Data-driven storytelling, 226
Data management systems, 208–209
Data privacy, *see* Privacy
Data quality, 179, 213
Davis, Angela, 33
Decision-making, 71, 135, 138, 211
DEI initiatives, 94, 105, 230–232
Democratization of philanthropy, 223–224
Demographics, donor, 81–82
Desired outcome, determining your, 116
Development, staff, 75
Digital security, trends in, 228–229
Diverse teams, 69–88. *See also* Unity in diversity
    action steps for creating, 85–86

budgetary considerations with, 80–81
case example, 76–77
challenges with, 78–79
creating an inclusive culture for, 75–76
ethical considerations with, 78–80
future trends, 81–85
and measuring diversity impact, 77–78
and power of diversity, 70–72
recruiting for, 72–75
Diversity. *See also* Unity in diversity
embracing, 54
power of, 70–72, 76–77
of supporters, 61
Docebo, 100
Doctors Without Borders, 97, 99
Donors:
AI and insights into, 168
authentic connections with, 71
balancing interests of communities
and, 59–60, 62
catering to egocentric preferences
of, 20, 21, 24*t*, 25
and communities, 41–42
demographics of, 81–82
discomfort of, with social justice
messaging, 40
at Earthjustice, 37
engagement and loyalty of, 18–19
managing perception of, 179
as partners, 34
in relationship fundraising, 8
and resistance to change, 198–199
satisfaction of, 17–18
types of, 18
understanding motives of, 19
and watchdog organizations, 6–7
Donor-advised funds (DAFs), 228
Donor-Centered Fundraising
(DCF), 15–29
action steps with, 28
bridging donor-centered and
community-centered, 49–50
case example, 19–20
community-centered fundraising vs., 11,
44, 45*t*–46*t*
and egocentrism, 24
and equity, 23
focus of, 11
and human-centered fundraising, 53
mistakes and pitfalls in, 22–23
moving beyond, 63
origins and evolution of, 5–7, 16
principles of, 16–18
relationship fundraising as, 8
research-based benefits of, 18–19

strengths and challenges of, 20–22, 21*t*
and technology, 26–28
unintended consequences of, 23–26
Donor Engagement platform, 175
Donor fatigue, 121–122, 236
Donor growth rate, 217
Donor journeys, personalized, 174
Donor lifetime value (LTV), 217
DonorPerfect, 99
Donor retention (donor retention rate),
138, 217, 228
Donor satisfaction and retention
metric, 204, 206
DonorSearch (software platform), 178
Drucker, Peter, 4, 145, 203

E
Earthjustice, 35–39
Economic justice, 35
Eden Projects, 207–208
Education nonprofits, 120, 136, 158, 208
Efficiency, improving, 58
Egocentrism, 24, 25
Email marketing, 155
Emotion AI, 184
Emotional connections, creating, 114
Emotional language, in storytelling, 117
Emotional regulation, 97
Empathy, 52, 148–149
Empowering storytelling, 115–116
Empowerment quotient, 204, 207
Environmental Defense Fund, 104
Environmental nonprofits, 119, 136, 158
Environmental sustainability, 84
Equity:
and donor-centered fundraising, 23
emphasis on, 84
fundraising grounded in, 34
and personalization, 50
as principle of human-centered
fundraising, 52
Estate planning, 234
Ethical considerations:
with AI, 170–173, 223
with diverse teams, 78–80
with donor-centered fundraising, 24
with human-centered fundraising, 62–63
with implementation, 154–157
with metrics, 215
Ethical storytelling, 115–116
Event conversion rate, 217
Event planning, AI-driven, 184
Expectations, donor, 17
Explainable AI (XAI), 171

F

Face-to-face interactions, 181
Failure, learning from, 153
Fairness, xvi, 171
Farrelly, Jono, 92
Feedback:
    constructive, 97
    learning from, 152–153
    for metrics, 209, 211
    as part of toolkit, 197
    stakeholder, 143–144
Feeding Futures, 212
Financial audits, 142–143
Financial metrics, 204–205
Flexibility, 75–76, 152
Flexible giving, 227
Focus groups, 152
Follow-ups, automated, 174
Forgotten Middle, 234
Fundraising, 3–13
    action steps with, 3–13
    agency-centered, 3–4
    historical context of, 4–5
    past and future of, 12–13
    relationship, 7–11
    supercharging, with AI, 167–168
Fundraising.AI, 148, 171
Fundraising Effectiveness Project (FEP), 142
Fundraising performance indicators, 77
Fundraising ROI, 217
Futureproofing, 72
Future trends, 221–239. *See also* AI
    action steps, 238
    challenges and pitfalls, 235–236
    chatbots and virtual assistants, 222–223
    cryptocurrency donations, 228
    DEI and anti-DEI initiatives, 230–232
    digital security, 228–229
    diverse teams, 81–85
    donor advised funds, 228
    donor retention, 228
    flexible giving, 227
    of fundraising, 12–13
    generational shifts, 234
    giving circles and collective-impact
        philanthropy, 223–225
    globalization, 232–233
    in implementation, 159–161
    integration with commerce, 227
    micro-donations, 226
    multi-level donor programs, 229
    non-cash gifts, 228
    personalization, 222, 227
    predictive analytics, 222
    recurrent giving and subscription models, 226
    regulatory landscape, 235

    social enterprises and hybrid models, 227–228
    storytelling, 225–226
    sustainability, 233–234
    transparency, 229–230

G

Gemini, 178
General Motors Foundation, xii
Generational shifts, 234
Generosity crisis, 166–167
Gen X, 234
Gen Z, 234
Gift frequency, 217
Girard, Joe, 3
GiveDirectly, 108
GiveSmart (software platform), 178
Giving analysis, 174
Giving circles, 223–225
Giving models, predictive, 183
Giving USA, 4
Global engagement, 83
GlobalGiving, 98, 100
Globalization, impact of, 232–233
Goals, 145, 175
Google Analytics, 123
Grapevine, 224
Grassroots Institute for Fundraising Training, 33
Gravyty (software platform), 178
Great Recession, xii
Green fundraising, 233
Greenpeace International, 6
Growth mindset, 97
GuideStar, 6

H

Haiti Partners Inc., 136
Hallowell, Edward M., 127
Harlem Children's Zone, 95
Healthcare nonprofits, 120, 136, 157, 208
Heartfelt Connector, 207
Hemachandra, Maya, 32, 35, 39, 40, 50
Heroism, collaborative, 91
Hiring practices, 74
Honesty, 154
Hootsuite, 124
Hope Community Services, 158–159
Hopeful Horizons, 98, 103–105
Human-centered design, 101
Human-centered fundraising, 51–66
    action steps with, 64–65
    benefits of, 58–59
    case examples, 56–58
    challenges and solutions in, 59–61
    and community-centered fundraising, 44,
        46–47, 54–55

embracing, 66
ethical considerations in, 62–63
greater impact through, 53–54
implementation of, xiv–xv
integrating, with organizational
    strategy, 61–62
leveraging technology and responsible
    AI for, 56
principles of, 52
Human-centered metrics, 208–209
"Human moment" (storytelling), 127
Human rights organizations, 120
Hyper-personalization, 183

I
Impact:
collective, 86–88
desire to make, xiv
greater, through human-centered
    fundraising, 53–54
measuring, 60
of storytelling, 61
Impact Online, 6
Impact reporting, 17
Implementation, 141–163
action steps for, 161–162
assessing current practices prior to, 142–144
and building your infrastructure, 147–149
case example, 158–159
challenges with, 149–150
checklist for, 153
and developing your strategy, 144–145
with digital/social media, 155–156
ethical considerations with, 154–157
flexibility with, 152
future trends in, 159–161
of human-centered fundraising, xiv–xv
and journey mapping, 145–147
lack of clear guidelines for, 42
and learning from feedback/failure, 152–153
refining your, 150–151
sector-specific considerations with, 157–158
INCITE! Women of Color Against Violence, 33
Inclusion:
culture of, for diverse teams, 75–76
embracing, 54
emphasis on, 84
fostering, 39, 58
in job descriptions, 73
as principle of human-centered fundraising, 52
India, 225
Influence, inequitable, 134–135
Infrastructure, building, 147–149
Injustice, systemic, 23
The Innocence Project, 208
Innovation, 71

Inspiration, xvi
Instagram, 225
Institute for Sustainable Philanthropy, 8
Institute of Museum and Library Services
    (IMLS), 105
Integration, 53, 166–167
Integrity, xvi
Interactive storytelling, 127
International fundraising laws, 235
International Rescue Committee, 123
IoT devices, 210, 215

J
James Beard Foundation, 57–58
Job descriptions, 73
Journey mapping, 145–147

K
Kennedy, John F., xiii
Kindsight (software platform), 178
Kiva, 233
Koshy, Cherian, 171, 210

L
Langley, Jim, 21, 25, 46
Le, Vu, xiv–xv, 31, 33, 43, 54
League of Heroes paradigm, 90
League of Heroes World Cup, 91–92
Learning:
culture of, 148–149
from feedback/failure, 152–153
as principle of human-centered fundraising, 52
LinkedIn, 73
Lives touched (metric), 204.205
Lorde, Audre, 33

M
McGill, Maia, 69, 195
Machine learning, 160
Marginalized communities, 23
Marginalized voices, amplifying, 137
Maslow, Abraham, 51
MAZON: A Jewish Response to Hunger, 147
Meltwater, 123
Memorial Sloan Kettering Cancer Center, 56–57
Mercy Ships Canada, 119
Metrics, 203–220
action steps with, 218–219
balanced scorecard, 201
best practices with, 217
case examples, 207–208, 212
challenges with, 213–214
complexity in, 40
deciding what to measure, 61–62
and defining success, 203–207

for diversity impact, 77–78
effectiveness of storytelling, 123–124
engagement, 123
ethical considerations with, 215
formulas, 217
future trends in, 216–217, 219–220
for impact, 60
leveraging, for growth, 212–213
of new types of impact, 150
quantitative vs. qualitative, 212
risk-adjusted, 214
and staff-volunteer engagement, 215–216
tracking human-centered, 208–209
for unity in diversity, 106–108
using technology with, 209–210, 214–215
Metric audits, 216
Michigan Department of Health and Human
    Services (MDHHS), 102
Micro-donations, 226
Microsoft Teams, 99
Millennials, 234
Miro, 99
Misconceptions, dispelling, 115
Mission, staying true to your, 25–26
Mission drift, 24, 60
Modern Institute for Charitable Giving, 148
Momentum (platform), 175
Momentum Nonprofit Productivity Report
    (2024), 169, 181
Monday.com, 98
Monthly giving and retention (metric), 206
Multi-level donor programs, 229
Munoz, Stephanie, 94
MURAL, 99

N
Narratives, compelling, 116–118
National Youth Orchestra of the UK, 10
Nature Conservancy, 96, 100, 119, 176, 229
Non-cash gifts, 228
Nonprofit AF (blog), 33
Non-Profit Anti-Racism Coalition, 33
Nonprofit Technology Network (NTEN), 148

O
Online donations, 6
Open communication, 152
Organizational culture, 19, 77, 200
Organizational sustainability, 19

P
Partnerships, purpose-driven, 46–47
Patagonia, 227
Peer-to-peer storytelling, 225

People's Institute for Survival and Beyond, 33
Personalization, 183
    and equity, 50
    as principle of donor-centered fundraising, 17
    in relationship fundraising, 8
    with technology, 82
    trends in, 222, 227
Personalized donor journeys, 174
Perspectives, bridging, 96, 114
Planned giving, 234
Powell, John A., 192, 197
Power (power dynamics), 131–140
    action steps with, 139–140
    addressing, in diverse teams, 80
    best practices for, 134
    challenges with, 134–135
    and decision-making, 138
    of diversity, 70–72, 76–77
    and empowerment via education, 139
    imbalances in, 24
    of integration, 53
    and resistance from stakeholders, 136–137
    role of technology in, 137–138
    sector-specific considerations with, 136, 139
    of storytelling, 114–115
    success metrics for, 138
Predictive analytics, 168–169, 222
Prisma Health Upstate, 19–20
Privacy (data privacy), 80, 170, 171, 178, 183, 215
Privilege, acknowledging, xi
Project Renewal, 119
Proposal writing, using AI for, 174
Prospect research, using AI for, 173–174
Purpose, shared, 50
Purpose-driven partnerships, 46–47

Q
Quantitative metrics, qualitative vs., 212

R
Rasmussen, Emily, 224
Reagan, Ronald, 4
Recruiting, for diverse teams, 72–75
Recurrent giving, 226
Recurring gift percentage, 217
Regulatory landscape, 235
Relationship fundraising, 7–11. *See also*
    Donor-centered fundraising
Remote work, 81
Representation, lack of, 135
Resistance to change, 191–202
    best practices and tools for handling, 197–199
    in building diverse teams, 78
    case examples, 196

common objections, addressing, 193–195
for community-centered fundraising, 40
current trends in, 199
and donor perspectives, 198–199
for human-centered fundraising, 59
and implementation, 149
and organizational leadership, 199
and sustainability, 200–201
and technology/resource constraints, 195–196
understanding roots of, 192–193
using storytelling to address, 200
Resources:
disparities in, 23
diverse sources of, 83
mobilizing, with human-centered
fundraising, 55
types of, 55
Resource constraints, 149, 213
in human-centered fundraising, 60
and resistance to change, 195–196
and storytelling, 121
Responsible AI, 56
Retaliation, fear of, 135
Retention rates, 61, 79
Ripple Effect Foundation, 207
Risks:
with AI, 182–183
of mission drift, 60
to revenues and donor relationships, 42
Risk-adjusted metrics, 214
Risk aversion, 180
Rockefeller Foundation, 105
Rogare, 43

S
St. John Fisher University, 173
St. Jude Children's Research Hospital, 120
Salesforce Einstein, 178
Salesforce Nonprofit Cloud, 99
Sargeant, Adrian, 8
Savior complexes, 23
Scaling, 43–44
Scripts, objection-handling, 198
Sector-specific considerations:
with implementation, 157–158
with power dynamics, 136, 139
with storytelling, 119–120
Selflessness, xvi
Self-reflection, xi–xii
Shang, Jen, 8
Sierra Club, 105
Similarity, 72
Sinek, Simon, 15
Slack, 99
Social justice, 34, 35, 40

Social Justice Fund Northwest, 33
Social media, 155–156
Social proof, 72
Staff:
and AI, 175, 179
and metrics, 215–216
storytelling by, 124–127
Stakeholders. *See also* Resistance to change
balancing needs of, 61, 150
buy-in from, 213
engagement of, 175, 211
feedback from, 143–144
resistance from, 136–137
satisfaction of, 61
StandTogether, 102
Stanford University, 171
Stereotypes, 115, 122–123
Stewardship, 17, 210
Story banks, 125
Storytelling, 113–129
action steps for, 127–128
to address resistance to change, 200
and AI, 177, 183
case examples, 118–119
challenges with, 120–122
and creating compelling narratives, 116–118
cultural sensitivity in, 122–123
data-driven, 226
engagement through, 59
ethical and empowering, 115–116
future trends in, 225–226
"human moment" in, 127
impact of, 61
and implementation, 154, 156–157
inclusive, 231
interactive, 127
measuring effectiveness of, 123–124
metrics for, 210–211
as part of toolkit, 197
power of, 114–115
sector-specific considerations with, 119–120
and unity in diversity, 100–103, 110–111
video, 126
by volunteers/staff, 124–127
Subscription models, 134, 226
Success, metrics for, 138, 203–207
Surveys, 152
Sustainability:
environmental, 84
future trends in, 233–234
and resistance to change, 200–201
Sweet, Leonard I., 221
Systemic inequalities, addressing, 231
Systemic injustice, 23
Systemic issues, 160

T
TalentLMS, 100
Teach for America, 120
Team(s):
    building, 197
    developing skills in your, 148
    diverse (*see* Diverse teams)
    dynamics of, 95–98
Team composition metrics, 77
Team Rubicon, 94
Technology:
    for collaboration, 224
    and donor-centered fundraising, 26–28
    for human-centered fundraising, 56
    investing in, 147–148
    for metrics, 209–210, 214–215
    overreliance on, 236
    as part of toolkit, 197
    personalization with, 82
    and power dynamics, 137–138
    in relationship fundraising, 8
    and resistance to change, 195–196
    and storytelling, 125–127
    and unity in diversity, 98–100
    use of, by nonprofits, 6
TikTok, 225
Tiltify, 225
Time, value of, 34, 37
Tokenism, 79–80
Tran, Lisa, 236
Transactional charity, 23
Transparency, 17, 39, 154, 170
    future trends in, 229–230
    and metrics, 211, 215
    and power dynamics, 136
    as principle of human-centered fundraising, 52
Trello, 98, 195
Trump administration, 94, 230
Trust, 115, 198

U
Unique value proposition, 115
United Way, xii, 101
Unity in diversity, 89–111
    actions steps for creating, 109–110
    case example, 91–92
    challenges in creating, 103–105

    and collaborative heroism, 91
    and collective impact, 86–88
    and current trends, 105–106
    and the greater good, xiii–xiv
    and League of Heroes paradigm, 90
    and storytelling, 100–103, 110–111
    strategies for, 92–95
    success metrics for, 106–108
    and team dynamics, 95–98
    and technology, 98–100
U.S. Census Bureau, 231
User-generated content, 225
UTM, 123

V
Values, living your, 72
Video storytelling, 126
Virtual assistants, 222–223
Virtual engagement, 83
Virtual events, 155
Virtual reality, 126–127, 184, 225
Virtuous (software platform), 177
Vision, human-centered, 144–145
Visual storytelling, 211
Voice recognition, 184
Volunteers:
    AI for managing, 176–177
    and diverse teams, 81
    and metrics, 215–216
    retention rate for, 61
    storytelling by, 124–127

W
Watchdog organizations, 6–7
WaterNet, 136
Way, Gerard, 141
Websites, 155
Western States Center, 33
White Pony Express, 7
Wilkins, Roger, 89
Women's Foundation of California, 224
Work, remote, 81
Working styles, 95–96

Z
Zero Gap Fund, 105
Zoom, 99